DR. HERMIONE MENDEZ

CKD

DIET COOKBOOK

FOR BEGINNERS

28-DAY
EASY-TO-FOLLOW
MEAL PLAN

CKD DIET

COOKBOOK FOR

BEGINNERS

The Ultimate Low-Salt, Low-Potassium, And Low-Phosphorus Recipes Guide To Healing From Chronic Kidney Disease Stage 3 & 4 With Simple Nutrition.

DR. HERMIONE MENDEZ

TABLE OF CONTENTS

INTRODUCTION

As I sit down to write this introduction, a wave of emotions engulfs me. It's a blend of gratitude, triumph, and a profound sense of purpose. You see, my life took an unexpected turn when I was diagnosed with Chronic Kidney Disease (CKD) in its formidable Stage 3. But through the power of proper dieting and determination, I not only survived but thrived. As a nutritionist, it is my heartfelt honor to share my story and the recipes that helped me reclaim my health in this CKD Diet Cookbook.

Like many others, I initially felt overwhelmed and frightened by the diagnosis. CKD can be a relentless adversary, demanding strict attention to diet and lifestyle choices. It was during those challenging moments that I decided to take control of my destiny and embark on a journey of resilience and renewal.

In the depths of my struggle, from what I have always known in my years of practice as a physician, I rediscovered that a well-crafted diet played a crucial role in managing CKD. Each meal became an opportunity to nourish my body, support my kidneys, and preserve my overall well-being. With the guidance of my colleagues and other healthcare professionals, diligent research, and unwavering determination, I developed a collection of recipes that not only met the stringent dietary requirements of CKD but also celebrated the joy of eating.

Within the pages of this cookbook, I invite you to join me on this transformative voyage. As you navigate through the recipes and delve into my personal anecdotes, I hope you find solace, inspiration, and, above all, a renewed sense of hope. Together, we will explore flavors, textures, and ingredients that nourish our bodies while satisfying our taste buds.

This cookbook goes beyond being a mere collection of recipes. It encapsulates the essence of my journey—a testament to the incredible power of the human spirit and the transformative impact of a well-planned diet. Each dish is imbued with intention, meticulously crafted to not only meet the dietary needs of CKD but to also ignite a passion for food and life.

As you immerse yourself in the pages that follow, allow yourself to be transported into a world where food becomes a source of healing and vitality. Relish the stories intertwined with the recipes, as they offer glimpses into the triumphs and setbacks I encountered along my path to wellness.

Remember, my dear reader, that this cookbook is not just a compilation of culinary creations; it is a testament to the strength of the human spirit and the boundless possibilities that lie within each of us. It is my sincerest wish that you find comfort, inspiration, and renewed hope within these pages. May they serve as a guiding light on your own journey toward resilience, renewal, and a vibrant life despite the challenges of CKD.

Together, let us embrace this culinary adventure, savoring each nourishing bite, and let our hearts be filled with gratitude for the gift of life and the transformative power of a properly tailored diet.

Chronic Kidney Disease (CKD) is a prevalent and serious condition that affects millions of people worldwide. In this chapter, we will delve into the intricacies of CKD, its impact on overall health, and the crucial role that diet plays in managing the condition effectively. With the right dietary approach, individuals with CKD can slow the progression of the disease, manage symptoms, and improve their quality of life.

UNDERSTANDING CHRONIC KIDNEY DISEASE (CKD):

CKD refers to the gradual loss of kidney function over time, resulting in the accumulation of waste products and fluid imbalances in the body. This condition can be caused by various factors, including diabetes, high blood pressure, genetic predisposition, and certain medications. As the kidneys' ability to filter waste and excess fluids diminishes, CKD progresses through different stages, ultimately leading to end-stage renal disease (ESRD), where dialysis or a kidney transplant becomes necessary.

IMPORTANCE OF DIET IN MANAGING CKD:

Diet plays a critical role in the management of CKD as it directly impacts the workload of the kidneys and helps control the buildup of waste and fluid in the body. A well-planned and individualized diet can help slow the progression of CKD, manage symptoms like high blood pressure and edema, and prevent complications such as cardiovascular disease and malnutrition.

Scientific data supports the significance of dietary modifications in CKD management. Studies have shown that adhering to a CKD-friendly diet can reduce the risk of kidney failure, improve overall kidney function, and enhance patients' well-being. A controlled diet can help regulate electrolyte levels, maintain a healthy blood pressure range, and prevent imbalances of minerals like potassium, phosphorus, and sodium. Additionally, proper nutrition can optimize protein intake, prevent muscle wasting, and promote a healthy weight, all of which are crucial for CKD patients.

GETTING STARTED WITH A CKD-FRIENDLY DIET:

Embarking on a CKD-friendly diet may initially seem overwhelming, but with the right guidance and knowledge, it can become a manageable and empowering lifestyle change. In this section, we will provide you with essential information to kick-start your journey towards a healthier diet for CKD.

- Consultation with a Healthcare Professional: It is essential to consult with a registered dietitian or healthcare professional specializing in CKD to assess your specific needs, stage of CKD, and individual health factors. They will create a personalized dietary plan tailored to your requirements, taking into account factors such as your current kidney function, nutritional status, medications, and dietary preferences.

- Controlling Protein Intake: Protein is a crucial nutrient for the body, but excessive consumption can put additional strain on the kidneys. Depending on the stage of CKD, your healthcare professional will provide protein recommendations to prevent malnutrition while minimizing kidney workload. They may suggest moderating the intake of high-quality proteins like lean meats, poultry, fish, and dairy products, and incorporating plant-based protein sources such as legumes, tofu, and quinoa.

- Managing Sodium and Fluid Intake: Sodium and fluid control are vital aspects of managing CKD-related complications like high blood pressure and fluid retention. Your healthcare professional will guide you in reducing sodium intake by limiting processed and packaged foods, avoiding excessive salt during cooking, and reading food labels carefully. They will also provide guidelines on fluid intake to prevent fluid overload and swelling, which can strain the kidneys and worsen symptoms.

- Monitoring Potassium and Phosphorus Levels: Imbalances in potassium and phosphorus can occur in CKD, leading to complications like electrolyte disturbances, muscle weakness, and bone disorders. Your healthcare professional will help you identify foods that are high in potassium and phosphorus, and advise on portion control and appropriate cooking techniques to minimize their intake.

- Balancing Macronutrients and Micronutrients: Achieving a balanced diet is essential for overall health and well-being. Your healthcare professional will guide you in balancing macronutrients (carbohydrates, proteins, and fats) to ensure adequate energy and nutrient intake. They will also provide recommendations for essential vitamins and minerals, such as vitamin D, calcium, and iron, which are crucial for bone health, anemia prevention, and immune function.

- Meal Planning and Portion Control: Planning meals in advance and practicing portion control can help maintain a healthy and consistent diet. Your healthcare professional will assist you in creating meal plans that align with your dietary restrictions and preferences, ensuring a variety of nutrient-dense foods to support your overall health.

Understanding CKD and the importance of a well-managed diet is vital for individuals with this condition. By following a CKD-friendly diet, you can help slow the progression of the disease, manage symptoms, and improve your quality of life. It is crucial to work closely with a healthcare professional specializing in CKD to receive personalized dietary guidance based on your specific needs. With the right knowledge and support, you can take control of your diet and embark on a path towards better kidney health and overall well-being.

CHAPTER 1: CKD DIET BASICS

RENAL DIET PRINCIPLES FOR CHRONIC KIDNEY DISEASE

Chronic Kidney Disease (CKD) is a condition characterized by the gradual loss of kidney function over time. It is essential for individuals with CKD to follow a specialized diet that supports kidney health, manages symptoms, and minimizes complications. In this chapter, we will explore the fundamental principles of a CKD diet, focusing on sodium restriction, potassium management, phosphorus control, and fluid intake guidelines.

SODIUM RESTRICTION: BALANCING BLOOD PRESSURE AND FLUID LEVELS

Sodium plays a crucial role in maintaining fluid balance and blood pressure regulation in the body. However, excessive sodium intake can lead to fluid retention and increased blood pressure, placing additional strain on the kidneys. For individuals with CKD, managing sodium intake is vital to prevent fluid overload and further kidney damage.

Current dietary guidelines recommend limiting sodium intake to 2,300 milligrams (mg) per day for the general population. However, for individuals with CKD, a more restrictive approach is often necessary. A sodium-restricted diet in CKD typically ranges between 1,500 and 2,000 mg per day, depending on the severity of kidney dysfunction.

Reducing sodium intake involves more than just avoiding table salt. Processed foods, such as canned soups, frozen meals, and packaged snacks, tend to be high in sodium. It is crucial to read food labels carefully and choose low-sodium or sodium-free alternatives. Fresh and minimally processed foods, seasoned with herbs and spices instead of salt, can add flavor without the sodium overload.

POTASSIUM MANAGEMENT: MAINTAINING ELECTROLYTE BALANCE

Potassium is an essential mineral involved in muscle function, nerve transmission, and maintaining electrolyte balance within the body. However, impaired kidney function can lead to potassium buildup in the blood, a condition known as hyperkalemia. Hyperkalemia can disrupt normal heart rhythm and pose serious health risks.

In CKD, potassium management is crucial. The recommended daily intake of potassium for individuals with CKD varies depending on the stage of the disease and the individual's specific needs. Typically, a moderate potassium restriction is advised, aiming for a daily intake of 2,000-3,000 mg.

High-potassium foods, such as bananas, oranges, potatoes, tomatoes, and beans, should be consumed in moderation. Instead, individuals with CKD can opt for low-potassium alternatives like apples, berries, cucumbers, and cauliflower. Cooking methods can also affect potassium content. Soaking vegetables in water before cooking and discarding the water can help reduce potassium levels.

PHOSPHORUS CONTROL: BALANCING MINERAL LEVELS

Phosphorus is a mineral that works closely with calcium to support bone health and other critical bodily functions. However, in CKD, the kidneys struggle to remove excess phosphorus, leading to its accumulation in the blood. Elevated phosphorus levels can contribute to bone and mineral disorders, cardiovascular complications, and further kidney damage.

Phosphorus control in a CKD diet involves limiting high-phosphorus foods such as dairy products, processed meats, nuts, and carbonated beverages. These items are typically rich in phosphorus additives that are more readily absorbed by the body. Choosing lower phosphorus alternatives like lean meats, poultry, fresh fruits, and vegetables can help maintain a balance.

Phosphorus binders may also be prescribed to individuals with advanced CKD to reduce phosphorus absorption. These medications bind to dietary phosphorus in the gastrointestinal tract, preventing its absorption into the bloodstream. It is essential to take these binders with meals as directed by a healthcare provider.

FLUID INTAKE GUIDELINES: MANAGING FLUID BALANCE

Maintaining adequate fluid balance is essential for individuals with CKD. Impaired kidney function can lead to reduced urine output, resulting in fluid retention. Proper fluid management is crucial to prevent edema, high blood pressure, and strain on the kidneys.

Fluid intake recommendations vary depending on the stage of CKD and the individual's specific needs. In early stages, fluid intake is typically unrestricted unless otherwise advised by a healthcare professional. However, as CKD progresses, fluid intake may need to be limited to prevent fluid overload.

Monitoring daily urine output can provide insights into fluid balance. Fluid restriction is typically recommended when urine output decreases significantly or when fluid overload symptoms, such as swelling or shortness of breath, occur. Healthcare providers may provide specific guidelines based on individual needs, considering factors such as urine output, blood pressure, and the presence of other health conditions.

It is essential to note that fluid restriction should be personalized and closely monitored under the guidance of a healthcare professional. Severe fluid restriction can lead to dehydration and other complications, so it is crucial to strike a balance that supports kidney function while maintaining proper hydration.

DR. HERMIONE MENDEZ

DIABETIC RENAL DIET

COOKBOOK FOR BEGINNERS

2000

days of recipes

100+

diabetes and kidney-friendly meals

30-DAY MEAL PLAN

CHAPTER 2: ESSENTIAL NUTRIENTS FOR KIDNEY HEALTH

The kidneys play a vital role in maintaining our overall health by filtering waste products and excess fluids from the bloodstream. When it comes to kidney health, it is crucial to provide the body with the right balance of nutrients to support optimal function and prevent complications. In this chapter, we will explore the essential nutrients that promote kidney health, including protein, healthy fats and oils, carbohydrates, vitamins and minerals, as well as antioxidants and phytochemicals.

PROTEIN REQUIREMENTS AND SOURCES

Protein is an essential nutrient that supports the growth, repair, and maintenance of tissues in the body. However, individuals with kidney disease often need to monitor their protein intake due to the kidneys' reduced ability to eliminate waste products generated by protein metabolism. The recommended protein intake for individuals with kidney disease varies depending on the stage of the condition and the individual's specific needs. Consultation with a healthcare professional or a registered dietitian is crucial for personalized protein recommendations.

When it comes to protein sources, it is essential to focus on high-quality proteins that are low in phosphorus and potassium. Some excellent sources of low-phosphorus and low-potassium protein include skinless poultry, fish, egg whites, and lean cuts of meat. Plant-based protein sources such as legumes, tofu, and quinoa can also be incorporated into the diet. These options provide essential amino acids while minimizing the burden on the kidneys.

HEALTHY FATS AND OILS

Healthy fats and oils play a crucial role in maintaining overall health, including kidney health. Omega-3 fatty acids, in particular, have been shown to have anti-inflammatory properties, which can help reduce inflammation in the kidneys and protect against kidney disease progression. Cold-water fatty fish like salmon, mackerel, and sardines are excellent sources of omega-3 fatty acids. Other sources include flaxseeds, chia seeds, and walnuts.

In addition to omega-3 fatty acids, monounsaturated fats, such as those found in olive oil, avocados, and nuts, can help promote heart health and reduce the risk of cardiovascular complications, which are often associated with kidney disease. It is important to consume these healthy fats in moderation, as they are calorie-dense and can contribute to weight gain if consumed excessively.

CARBOHYDRATES FOR ENERGY

Carbohydrates are the body's primary source of energy, and it is essential to choose the right type and amount of carbohydrates to support kidney health. Complex carbohydrates, such as whole grains, legumes, and vegetables, provide a slow and steady release of energy, preventing blood sugar spikes and promoting satiety.

Individuals with kidney disease should be cautious about their carbohydrate intake, particularly if they have diabetes or impaired glucose tolerance. Monitoring portion sizes and selecting carbohydrates with a low glycemic index can help maintain stable blood sugar levels and minimize stress on the kidneys. Examples of low glycemic index carbohydrates include whole wheat bread, quinoa, sweet potatoes, and non-starchy vegetables like broccoli and spinach.

VITAMINS AND MINERALS

Vitamins and minerals play a crucial role in maintaining overall health and supporting kidney function. However, individuals with kidney disease may have altered vitamin and mineral levels, and certain vitamins and minerals may need to be limited or supplemented. It is important to work closely with a healthcare professional or registered dietitian to ensure appropriate vitamin and mineral intake.

Some key vitamins and minerals for kidney health include:

- Vitamin D: Adequate vitamin D levels are essential for maintaining bone health and reducing the risk of complications such as renal osteodystrophy. Sun exposure and vitamin D-rich foods like fatty fish, fortified dairy products, and egg yolks can contribute to vitamin D levels.

- B Vitamins: B vitamins, including B6, B12, and folic acid, are important for red blood cell production and nerve function. Some kidney-friendly sources of B vitamins include whole grains, lean meats, eggs, and leafy green vegetables.

- Potassium: While potassium is an essential mineral, individuals with kidney disease may need to limit their potassium intake, as high levels can be harmful. Potassium-rich foods like bananas, oranges, potatoes, and tomatoes should be consumed in moderation.

- Phosphorus: High levels of phosphorus can lead to complications in kidney disease. Limiting phosphorus-rich foods like dairy products, processed meats, and certain carbonated beverages can help manage phosphorus levels.

ANTIOXIDANTS AND PHYTOCHEMICALS

Antioxidants and phytochemicals are compounds found in plant-based foods that help protect cells from damage caused by harmful free radicals. These compounds have been associated with a reduced risk of chronic diseases, including kidney disease. Including a variety of colorful fruits and vegetables in the diet can provide a wide range of antioxidants and phytochemicals.

Some examples of antioxidant-rich foods include berries (such as blueberries, strawberries, and raspberries), dark leafy greens (like spinach and kale), colorful bell peppers, tomatoes, and citrus fruits. These foods not only provide antioxidants but also contribute to overall hydration and are often low in potassium and phosphorus.

Incorporating these nutrient-rich foods into a kidney-friendly diet can provide a wide array of health benefits, including reduced inflammation, improved antioxidant status, and enhanced overall kidney function.

CHAPTER 3: BUILDING A CKD-FRIENDLY MEAL PLAN

Chronic Kidney Disease (CKD) requires careful management of diet to promote kidney health and overall well-being. In this chapter, we will explore the essential elements of a CKD-friendly meal plan, including meal planning strategies, portion control, grocery shopping tips, meal prepping, and dining out with CKD. By understanding and implementing these strategies, you can optimize your nutrition while effectively managing CKD.

MEAL PLANNING STRATEGIES:

Developing a meal plan tailored to your specific needs is crucial for individuals with CKD. A well-planned diet can help control blood pressure, maintain proper fluid balance, and manage electrolyte levels. Here are some key strategies to consider when building a CKD-friendly meal plan:

- Consult with a Registered Dietitian (RD): Working with an RD who specializes in kidney health is invaluable. They can assess your individual nutritional needs, provide personalized recommendations, and assist in creating a meal plan that aligns with your CKD stage, medications, and lifestyle.

- Limit Sodium Intake: High sodium intake can contribute to fluid retention and increased blood pressure, placing additional strain on the kidneys. Reduce your sodium intake by choosing fresh, whole foods over processed and packaged items. Flavor your meals with herbs, spices, and other low-sodium seasonings instead of relying on salt.

- Control Protein Intake: Depending on your CKD stage, protein restriction may be necessary to reduce the workload on your kidneys. Consult with your RD to determine the appropriate amount of protein for your condition. Opt for high-quality protein sources such as lean meats, poultry, fish, eggs, and plant-based options like legumes and tofu.

- Monitor Potassium and Phosphorus Levels: CKD can disrupt the balance of potassium and phosphorus in your body. Excess levels can lead to complications such as muscle weakness, bone disease, and irregular heart rhythms. Work with your RD to identify foods that are low in potassium and phosphorus and incorporate them into your meal plan.

PORTION CONTROL:

Controlling portion sizes is essential for managing CKD. Monitoring your intake helps maintain a balance of nutrients, prevents overconsumption, and assists in weight management. Consider the following tips for portion control:

- Use Measuring Tools: Invest in measuring cups, spoons, and a kitchen scale to accurately measure portion sizes. This will help you maintain consistency in your meal plan and prevent excessive consumption of certain nutrients.

- Create a Balanced Plate: Divide your plate into sections to guide portion sizes. Fill half of your plate with non-starchy vegetables like leafy greens, broccoli, and bell peppers. Allocate a quarter for lean protein sources and the remaining quarter for whole grains or starchy vegetables.

- Be Mindful of Liquid Intake: Fluid control is essential for individuals with CKD, especially if you are experiencing fluid retention or have been advised to limit fluid intake. Measure your liquids and consider consuming them at specific times throughout the day to maintain a balance.

GROCERY SHOPPING TIPS:

Navigating the grocery store aisles can be overwhelming, but with some helpful tips, you can make CKD-friendly choices and select nutrient-dense foods. Consider the following when grocery shopping:

- Read Food Labels: Pay attention to the nutritional information and ingredient list on food labels. Look for low-sodium options, and be aware of hidden sources of sodium such as monosodium glutamate (MSG) or sodium bicarbonate.
- Choose Fresh and Whole Foods: Opt for fresh fruits, vegetables, and whole grains whenever possible. These choices are naturally low in sodium, high in essential nutrients, and contribute to overall kidney health.
- Plan Ahead: Create a shopping list based on your meal plan to stay organized and focused while shopping. This helps avoid impulse purchases of foods that may not align with your CKD-friendly diet.

MEAL PREPPING FOR SUCCESS:

Meal prepping is a powerful tool for individuals with CKD. It saves time, ensures consistent adherence to dietary recommendations, and reduces the temptation to rely on convenience foods that may be less kidney-friendly. Consider the following tips for successful meal prepping:

- Choose Kidney-Friendly Recipes: Select recipes that align with your dietary restrictions and CKD stage. Look for meals that incorporate low-sodium ingredients, controlled protein portions, and limited potassium and phosphorus sources.

- Batch Cooking: Prepare larger quantities of kidney-friendly recipes and portion them into individual servings. Store these meals in the refrigerator or freezer for easy access during busy days.

- Use Appropriate Storage Containers: Invest in containers that are suitable for freezing, microwaving, and dishwasher-safe. Label them with the date and contents for easy identification.

DINING OUT WITH CKD:

Eating out can be challenging for individuals with CKD, as restaurant meals often contain hidden sodium, high levels of potassium, and excessive protein portions. However, with careful planning and communication, you can still enjoy dining out while adhering to your CKD-friendly diet:

- Research and Choose Restaurants Wisely: Look for restaurants that offer healthier options and are willing to accommodate special dietary needs. Many establishments have nutrition information available online or upon request, allowing you to make informed choices.

- Communicate with the Server: Inform your server about your dietary restrictions and request modifications to your meal, such as omitting high-sodium ingredients or preparing sauces on the side. Most restaurants are willing to accommodate special requests.

- Portion Control: Consider sharing a meal with a dining partner or ask for a take-out container at the beginning of the meal to portion out a suitable amount. This helps prevent overeating and allows you to enjoy the leftovers at a later time.

By implementing these strategies for building a CKD-friendly meal plan, controlling portion sizes, navigating grocery shopping, meal prepping, and dining out, you can effectively manage your condition and promote kidney health. Remember, it is essential to consult with a healthcare professional or a registered dietitian who specializes in CKD to tailor these strategies to your individual needs.

CHAPTER 4: DELICIOUS BREAKFAST RECIPES:

VEGETABLE EGG WHITE OMELET

Time: 15 minutes

Servings: 1

Ingredients:

- 4 egg whites
- 1/4 cup diced bell peppers
- 1/4 cup diced onions
- 1/4 cup chopped spinach
- 1/4 cup sliced mushrooms
- Salt and pepper to taste
- 1 teaspoon olive oil

Directions:

- Heat olive oil in a non-stick skillet over medium heat.
- Add onions, bell peppers, mushrooms, and spinach to the skillet. Sauté until vegetables are tender.

- In a bowl, whisk the egg whites until frothy. Season with salt and pepper.
- Pour the egg whites over the sautéed vegetables in the skillet.
- Cook for a few minutes until the edges are set, then gently lift the edges with a spatula and tilt the skillet to allow uncooked egg whites to flow to the edges.
- Once the omelet is mostly set, fold it in half and cook for an additional minute.
- Slide the omelet onto a plate and serve hot.

Nutritional Information:

- Calories: 150
- Protein: 20g
- Carbohydrates: 10g
- Fat: 3g
- Fiber: 3g

LOW-SODIUM BREAKFAST BURRITO WITH LEAN TURKEY

Time: 20 minutes

Servings: 1

Ingredients:

- 2 large lettuce leaves or low-sodium whole wheat tortillas
- 3 ounces lean ground turkey
- 1/4 cup diced tomatoes
- 2 tablespoons diced onions
- 2 tablespoons diced bell peppers
- 1/4 teaspoon chili powder
- 1/4 teaspoon cumin
- Salt and pepper to taste
- 1 teaspoon olive oil
- 2 tablespoons low-sodium salsa (optional)

Directions:

- Heat olive oil in a skillet over medium heat.
- Add onions, bell peppers, and ground turkey to the skillet. Cook until the turkey is browned and cooked through.
- Add diced tomatoes, chili powder, cumin, salt, and pepper to the skillet. Cook for an additional 2-3 minutes to allow flavors to meld.
- If using lettuce leaves, place the turkey mixture in the center of each leaf. If using tortillas, spread the turkey mixture in the center of each tortilla.
- If desired, top with low-sodium salsa.

- Roll up the lettuce leaves or tortillas to form a burrito.
- Serve immediately.

Nutritional Information:

- Calories: 250
- Protein: 25g
- Carbohydrates: 10g
- Fat: 10g
- Fiber: 2g

BUCKWHEAT PANCAKES WITH FRESH BERRIES

Time: 30 minutes

Servings: 2

Ingredients:

- 1 cup buckwheat flour
- 1 tablespoon baking powder
- 1 tablespoon sugar substitute
- 1/4 teaspoon salt
- 1 cup unsweetened almond milk
- 1 egg
- 1 teaspoon vanilla extract

- Fresh berries for topping (e.g., strawberries, blueberries, raspberries)

Directions:

- In a mixing bowl, whisk together buckwheat flour, baking powder, sugar substitute, and salt.
- In a separate bowl, whisk together almond milk, egg, and vanilla extract.
- Pour the wet ingredients into the dry ingredients and stir until just combined. Do not overmix; a few lumps are okay.
- Preheat a non-stick skillet or griddle over medium heat and lightly grease with cooking spray or a small amount of oil.
- Pour 1/4 cup of the pancake batter onto the skillet for each pancake. Cook until bubbles form on the surface, then flip and cook for another 1-2 minutes until golden brown.
- Repeat with the remaining batter.
- Serve the pancakes topped with fresh berries.

Nutritional Information:

- Calories: 200
- Protein: 8g
- Carbohydrates: 40g
- Fat: 3g
- Fiber: 6g

QUINOA BREAKFAST BOWL WITH APPLES AND CINNAMON

Time: 25 minutes

Servings: 2

Ingredients:

- 1 cup cooked quinoa
- 1 medium apple, diced
- 2 tablespoons chopped walnuts
- 1/2 teaspoon cinnamon
- 1/4 cup unsweetened almond milk
- 1 tablespoon honey or sugar substitute (optional)

Directions:

- In a bowl, combine cooked quinoa, diced apple, chopped walnuts, and cinnamon.
- Stir in almond milk and sweetener, if desired.
- Microwave the mixture for 1-2 minutes to warm it up.
- Divide the quinoa mixture into two bowls.
- Serve warm.

Nutritional Information:

- Calories: 220
- Protein: 5g
- Carbohydrates: 35g
- Fat: 8g
- Fiber: 6g

CHIA SEED PUDDING WITH ALMOND MILK AND FRESH FRUIT

Time: 5 minutes (plus overnight refrigeration)

Servings: 2

Ingredients:

- 1/4 cup chia seeds
- 1 cup unsweetened almond milk
- 1 tablespoon honey or sugar substitute
- 1/2 teaspoon vanilla extract
- Fresh fruit for topping (e.g., berries, sliced bananas)

Directions:

- In a bowl, whisk together chia seeds, almond milk, honey or sugar substitute, and vanilla extract.

- Cover the bowl and refrigerate overnight or for at least 4 hours until the mixture thickens and becomes pudding-like.
- Stir the chia seed pudding before serving to ensure even consistency.
- Divide the pudding into two serving bowls.
- Top with fresh fruit.

Nutritional Information:

- Calories: 150
- Protein: 4g
- Carbohydrates: 16g
- Fat: 8g
- Fiber: 10g

GREEK YOGURT PARFAIT WITH LOW-POTASSIUM FRUITS

Time: 10 minutes

Servings: 1

Ingredients:

- 1/2 cup low-potassium fruits (e.g., strawberries, blueberries, raspberries)

- 1/2 cup plain Greek yogurt
- 1 tablespoon chopped almonds or walnuts
- 1 teaspoon honey or sugar substitute

Directions:

- In a glass or bowl, layer low-potassium fruits, Greek yogurt, and chopped almonds or walnuts.
- Drizzle honey or sprinkle sugar substitute over the top.
- Repeat the layers if desired.
- Serve chilled.

Nutritional Information:

- Calories: 150
- Protein: 15g
- Carbohydrates: 10g
- Fat: 6g
- Fiber: 3g

SPINACH AND MUSHROOM FRITTATA

Time: 30 minutes

Servings: 4

Ingredients:

- 1 tablespoon olive oil
- 1 cup sliced mushrooms
- 2 cups fresh spinach
- 6 eggs
- 1/4 cup unsweetened almond milk
- Salt and pepper to taste
- 1/4 cup grated low-sodium cheese (optional)

Directions:

- Preheat the oven to 350°F (175°C).
- Heat olive oil in an oven-safe skillet over medium heat.
- Add sliced mushrooms to the skillet and cook until softened.
- Add fresh spinach to the skillet and cook until wilted.
- In a bowl, whisk together eggs, almond milk, salt, and pepper.
- Pour the egg mixture over the cooked mushrooms and spinach in the skillet.
- Cook on the stovetop for a few minutes until the edges start to set.
- Sprinkle grated cheese over the top, if desired.
- Transfer the skillet to the preheated oven and bake for 15-20 minutes until the frittata is set and slightly golden on top.

- Remove from the oven and let it cool for a few minutes before slicing.
- Serve warm or at room temperature.

Nutritional Information:

- Calories: 150
- Protein: 12g
- Carbohydrates: 3g
- Fat: 10g
- Fiber: 1g

OATMEAL WITH FLAXSEEDS AND SLICED BANANAS

Time: 10 minutes

Servings: 1

Ingredients:

- 1/2 cup old-fashioned oats
- 1 cup water
- 1 tablespoon ground flaxseeds
- 1/2 teaspoon cinnamon
- 1/2 banana, sliced
- 1 tablespoon chopped walnuts or almonds

- 1 teaspoon honey or sugar substitute

Directions:

- In a saucepan, bring water to a boil.
- Stir in oats, ground flaxseeds, and cinnamon.
- Reduce heat to low and simmer for about 5 minutes, stirring occasionally, until the oats are cooked and the mixture thickens.
- Remove from heat and let it cool slightly.
- Top the oatmeal with sliced bananas, chopped walnuts or almonds, and drizzle with honey or sprinkle with sugar substitute.
- Serve warm.

Nutritional Information:

- Calories: 200
- Protein: 6g
- Carbohydrates: 30g
- Fat: 7g
- Fiber: 5g

WHOLE WHEAT TOAST WITH AVOCADO AND POACHED EGG

Time: 15 minutes

Servings: 1

Ingredients:

- 1 slice whole wheat bread, toasted
- 1/2 avocado, mashed
- 1 poached egg
- Salt and pepper to taste
- 1 teaspoon chopped fresh cilantro or parsley (optional)

Directions:

- Spread mashed avocado on the toasted whole wheat bread.
- Place the poached egg on top of the avocado.
- Sprinkle with salt, pepper, and chopped fresh cilantro or parsley, if desired.
- Serve immediately.

Nutritional Information:

- Calories: 250
- Protein: 10g
- Carbohydrates: 20g
- Fat: 15g
- Fiber: 8g

SWEET POTATO HASH BROWNS WITH TURKEY BACON

Time: 30 minutes

Servings: 2

Ingredients:

- 1 medium sweet potato, peeled and grated
- 2 slices turkey bacon, chopped
- 1/4 cup diced onions
- 1/4 teaspoon paprika
- Salt and pepper to taste
- Cooking spray

Directions:

- Preheat the oven to 400°F (200°C).
- In a skillet, cook the turkey bacon until crispy. Remove from the skillet and set aside.
- Spray the skillet with cooking spray and add diced onions. Sauté until translucent.
- Add grated sweet potato, paprika, salt, and pepper to the skillet. Cook for about 10 minutes until the sweet potato is tender and slightly crispy, stirring occasionally.

- Stir in the cooked turkey bacon.
- Transfer the mixture to a baking sheet lined with parchment paper.
- Bake in the preheated oven for about 10-15 minutes until the hash browns are crispy.
- Remove from the oven and serve hot.

Nutritional Information:

- Calories: 180
- Protein: 8g
- Carbohydrates: 25g
- Fat: 6g
- Fiber: 4g

CHAPTER 5: SATISFYING LUNCH AND DINNER RECIPES

GRILLED LEMON HERB CHICKEN WITH STEAMED BROCCOLI:

Preparation time: 15 minutes

Cooking time: 25 minutes

Servings: 4

Ingredients:

- 4 boneless, skinless chicken breasts
- 2 lemons, juiced and zested
- 2 tablespoons olive oil
- 2 cloves garlic, minced
- 1 tablespoon fresh rosemary, chopped
- 1 tablespoon fresh thyme, chopped
- Salt and pepper to taste
- 4 cups broccoli florets

Directions:

- Preheat the grill to medium-high heat.
- In a small bowl, combine the lemon juice, lemon zest, olive oil, minced garlic, rosemary, thyme, salt, and pepper.
- Place the chicken breasts in a shallow dish and pour the marinade over them. Make sure the chicken is coated evenly. Let it marinate for 10 minutes.
- Grill the chicken breasts for about 6-8 minutes per side or until the internal temperature reaches 165°F (74°C).
- While the chicken is grilling, steam the broccoli florets for about 5 minutes or until tender.
- Serve the grilled lemon herb chicken with steamed broccoli on the side.

Nutritional information per serving:

- Calories: 250
- Protein: 30g
- Carbohydrates: 10g
- Fat: 10g
- Sodium: 100mg
- Potassium: 400mg

Note: The sodium and potassium content may vary depending on the specific ingredients used. Adjust the seasonings and marinade according to your dietary needs.

BAKED SALMON WITH DILL SAUCE AND ROASTED ASPARAGUS:

Preparation time: 10 minutes

Cooking time: 20 minutes

Servings: 4

Ingredients:

- 4 salmon fillets
- 2 tablespoons fresh dill, chopped
- 2 tablespoons lemon juice
- 1 tablespoon Dijon mustard
- 1 tablespoon olive oil
- Salt and pepper to taste
- 1 bunch asparagus, trimmed

For the Dill Sauce:

- 1/2 cup plain Greek yogurt

- 1 tablespoon fresh dill, chopped
- 1 tablespoon lemon juice
- Salt and pepper to taste

Directions:

- Preheat the oven to 400°F (200°C).
- Place the salmon fillets in a baking dish. In a small bowl, combine the chopped dill, lemon juice, Dijon mustard, olive oil, salt, and pepper. Spread this mixture over the salmon fillets.
- Arrange the asparagus on a separate baking sheet. Drizzle with olive oil, salt, and pepper.
- Bake the salmon and asparagus in the preheated oven for about 15-20 minutes, or until the salmon is cooked through and flakes easily with a fork.
- Meanwhile, prepare the dill sauce by combining the Greek yogurt, fresh dill, lemon juice, salt, and pepper in a small bowl. Mix well.
- Serve the baked salmon with dill sauce and roasted asparagus on the side.

Nutritional information per serving:

- Calories: 300
- Protein: 30g
- Carbohydrates: 8g

- Fat: 15g
- Sodium: 120mg
- Potassium: 550mg

TURKEY MEATBALLS WITH MARINARA SAUCE AND ZUCCHINI NOODLES:

Preparation time: 15 minutes

Cooking time: 25 minutes

Servings: 4

Ingredients:

- 1 pound ground turkey
- 1/4 cup breadcrumbs (low-sodium)
- 1/4 cup grated Parmesan cheese
- 1/4 cup chopped parsley
- 2 cloves garlic, minced
- 1/2 teaspoon dried oregano
- 1/2 teaspoon dried basil
- Salt and pepper to taste
- 2 cups low-sodium marinara sauce
- 4 medium zucchini, spiralized into noodles

- 1 tablespoon olive oil

Directions:

- Preheat the oven to 375°F (190°C).
- In a large bowl, combine the ground turkey, breadcrumbs, Parmesan cheese, chopped parsley, minced garlic, dried oregano, dried basil, salt, and pepper. Mix well.
- Shape the turkey mixture into meatballs of desired size and place them on a baking sheet lined with parchment paper.
- Bake the meatballs in the preheated oven for about 20-25 minutes, or until cooked through.
- While the meatballs are baking, heat olive oil in a large skillet over medium heat. Add the zucchini noodles and sauté for about 3-4 minutes until tender.
- In a separate saucepan, heat the marinara sauce over low heat until warmed.
- Serve the turkey meatballs with marinara sauce over the zucchini noodles.

Nutritional information per serving:

- Calories: 280
- Protein: 25g
- Carbohydrates: 15g
- Fat: 12g

- Sodium: 200mg
- Potassium: 550mg

Note: Adjust the seasoning and portion sizes according to your dietary needs.

SHRIMP STIR-FRY WITH BELL PEPPERS AND SNOW PEAS:

Preparation time: 10 minutes

Cooking time: 10 minutes

Servings: 4

Ingredients:

- 1 pound medium shrimp, peeled and deveined
- 2 tablespoons low-sodium soy sauce
- 1 tablespoon cornstarch
- 1 tablespoon sesame oil
- 1 tablespoon vegetable oil
- 1 red bell pepper, sliced
- 1 yellow bell pepper, sliced
- 1 cup snow peas
- 2 cloves garlic, minced

- 1 teaspoon grated fresh ginger
- Salt and pepper to taste
- Chopped green onions for garnish

Directions:

- In a small bowl, whisk together the soy sauce and cornstarch until smooth. Set aside.
- In a large skillet or wok, heat the sesame oil and vegetable oil over medium-high heat.
- Add the shrimp to the skillet and stir-fry for 2-3 minutes until they turn pink and opaque. Remove the shrimp from the skillet and set aside.
- In the same skillet, add the sliced bell peppers, snow peas, minced garlic, and grated ginger. Stir-fry for 3-4 minutes until the vegetables are crisp-tender.
- Return the shrimp to the skillet and pour in the soy sauce and cornstarch mixture. Stir-fry for another 1-2 minutes until the sauce thickens and coats the shrimp and vegetables.
- Season with salt and pepper to taste.
- Garnish with chopped green onions and serve the shrimp stir-fry over steamed rice or quinoa.

Nutritional information per serving:

- Calories: 200

- Protein: 25g
- Carbohydrates: 10g
- Fat: 6g
- Sodium: 350mg
- Potassium: 400mg

LENTIL AND VEGETABLE CURRY WITH BROWN RICE:

Preparation time: 15 minutes

Cooking time: 30 minutes

Servings: 4

Ingredients:

- 1 cup brown lentils
- 1 tablespoon vegetable oil
- 1 onion, chopped
- 2 cloves garlic, minced
- 1 tablespoon grated fresh ginger
- 1 tablespoon curry powder
- 1 teaspoon ground cumin
- 1 teaspoon ground coriander
- 1/2 teaspoon turmeric

- 1/4 teaspoon cayenne pepper (optional, adjust to taste)
- 2 carrots, diced
- 1 zucchini, diced
- 1 red bell pepper, diced
- 1 can (14 ounces) diced tomatoes (low-sodium)
- 1 can (14 ounces) coconut milk (light)
- Salt and pepper to taste
- Fresh cilantro for garnish
- Cooked brown rice for serving

Directions:

- Rinse the brown lentils under cold water and set aside.
- In a large pot, heat the vegetable oil over medium heat. Add the chopped onion, minced garlic, and grated ginger. Sauté for 2-3 minutes until the onion becomes translucent.
- Add the curry powder, ground cumin, ground coriander, turmeric, and cayenne pepper (if using). Stir to coat the onion mixture with the spices and cook for another minute.
- Add the diced carrots, zucchini, red bell pepper, diced tomatoes (with their juices), and brown lentils to the pot. Stir well to combine.
- Pour in the coconut milk and bring the mixture to a boil. Reduce the heat to low, cover the pot, and simmer for about 20-25 minutes until the lentils and vegetables are tender.

- Season with salt and pepper to taste.
- Serve the lentil and vegetable curry over cooked brown rice. Garnish with fresh cilantro.

Nutritional information per serving:

- Calories: 350
- Protein: 12g
- Carbohydrates: 50g
- Fat: 12g
- Sodium: 150mg
- Potassium: 700mg

QUINOA STUFFED BELL PEPPERS WITH TOMATO SAUCE:

Preparation time: 15 minutes

Cooking time: 35 minutes

Servings: 4

Ingredients:

- 4 bell peppers (any color), tops removed and seeds discarded
- 1 cup cooked quinoa

- 1/2 cup low-sodium black beans, rinsed and drained
- 1/2 cup corn kernels (fresh or frozen)
- 1/2 cup diced tomatoes
- 1/4 cup diced red onion
- 2 cloves garlic, minced
- 1 teaspoon ground cumin
- 1/2 teaspoon smoked paprika
- Salt and pepper to taste
- 1 cup low-sodium tomato sauce

Directions:

- Preheat the oven to 375°F (190°C).
- In a large bowl, combine the cooked quinoa, black beans, corn kernels, diced tomatoes, diced red onion, minced garlic, ground cumin, smoked paprika, salt, and pepper. Mix well.
- Stuff the bell peppers with the quinoa mixture and place them in a baking dish.
- Pour the tomato sauce over the stuffed bell peppers.
- Cover the baking dish with foil and bake in the preheated oven for about 30-35 minutes until the bell peppers are tender.
- Remove the foil and bake for an additional 5 minutes to allow the tops to slightly brown.
- Serve the quinoa stuffed bell peppers with tomato sauce.

Nutritional information per serving:

- Calories: 250
- Protein: 10g
- Carbohydrates: 50g
- Fat: 2g
- Sodium: 250mg
- Potassium: 500mg

Note: Adjust the seasonings and portion sizes according to your dietary needs.

GRILLED TOFU SKEWERS WITH TERIYAKI GLAZE AND GRILLED VEGETABLES:

Preparation time: 20 minutes

Cooking time: 10 minutes

Servings: 4

Ingredients:

- 1 block (14 ounces) firm tofu, drained and cut into cubes
- 1/4 cup low-sodium soy sauce

- 2 tablespoons rice vinegar
- 1 tablespoon honey
- 1 tablespoon grated fresh ginger
- 2 cloves garlic, minced
- 1 tablespoon sesame oil
- Assorted vegetables for grilling (such as bell peppers, zucchini, mushrooms, and red onion)
- Wooden skewers, soaked in water for 30 minutes
- Sesame seeds for garnish

Directions:

- In a bowl, whisk together the soy sauce, rice vinegar, honey, grated ginger, minced garlic, and sesame oil to make the teriyaki glaze.
- Thread the tofu cubes onto the soaked wooden skewers. Place the skewers in a shallow dish and pour the teriyaki glaze over them. Let them marinate for 10 minutes.
- Preheat the grill to medium-high heat.
- Meanwhile, prepare the vegetables by cutting them into skewer-friendly pieces.
- Grill the tofu skewers and vegetables for about 4-5 minutes per side or until grill marks appear and the vegetables are tender.
- Remove the skewers from the grill and sprinkle with sesame seeds.

- Serve the grilled tofu skewers with teriyaki glaze alongside the grilled vegetables.

Nutritional information per serving:

- Calories: 180
- Protein: 12g
- Carbohydrates: 15g
- Fat: 8g
- Sodium: 250mg
- Potassium: 300mg

BAKED COD WITH LEMON AND HERBS SERVED WITH STEAMED SPINACH:

Preparation time: 10 minutes

Cooking time: 15 minutes

Servings: 4

Ingredients:

- 4 cod fillets
- 2 tablespoons lemon juice
- 2 tablespoons olive oil

- 1 tablespoon chopped fresh parsley
- 1 teaspoon chopped fresh dill
- 1 teaspoon chopped fresh thyme
- Salt and pepper to taste
- 4 cups fresh spinach

Directions:

- Preheat the oven to 400°F (200°C).
- Place the cod fillets in a baking dish.
- In a small bowl, whisk together the lemon juice, olive oil, chopped parsley, chopped dill, chopped thyme, salt, and pepper.
- Pour the lemon and herb mixture over the cod fillets, making sure they are well coated.
- Bake the cod in the preheated oven for about 12-15 minutes or until the fish is opaque and flakes easily with a fork.
- While the cod is baking, steam the spinach for about 3-4 minutes until wilted.
- Serve the baked cod with lemon and herbs on a bed of steamed spinach.

Nutritional information per serving:

- Calories: 150
- Protein: 25g
- Carbohydrates: 2g

- Fat: 5g
- Sodium: 150mg
- Potassium: 600mg

CHICKEN AND VEGETABLE STIR-FRY WITH LOW-SODIUM SOY SAUCE:

Preparation time: 15 minutes

Cooking time: 15 minutes

Servings: 4

Ingredients:

- 1 pound boneless, skinless chicken breasts, sliced into thin strips
- 2 tablespoons low-sodium soy sauce
- 1 tablespoon cornstarch
- 1 tablespoon vegetable oil
- 2 cloves garlic, minced
- 1 tablespoon grated fresh ginger
- 1 red bell pepper, sliced
- 1 yellow bell pepper, sliced
- 1 cup snow peas
- 1 cup sliced mushrooms

- 2 green onions, chopped
- Salt and pepper to taste

Directions:

- In a small bowl, whisk together the soy sauce and cornstarch until smooth. Set aside.
- Heat the vegetable oil in a large skillet or wok over medium-high heat.
- Add the sliced chicken to the skillet and stir-fry for 3-4 minutes until cooked through. Remove the chicken from the skillet and set aside.
- In the same skillet, add the minced garlic and grated ginger. Sauté for about 1 minute until fragrant.
- Add the sliced bell peppers, snow peas, sliced mushrooms, and chopped green onions to the skillet. Stir-fry for 3-4 minutes until the vegetables are crisp-tender.
- Return the cooked chicken to the skillet and pour in the soy sauce and cornstarch mixture. Stir-fry for another 1-2 minutes until the sauce thickens and coats the chicken and vegetables.
- Season with salt and pepper to taste.
- Serve the chicken and vegetable stir-fry over steamed rice or cauliflower rice.

Nutritional information per serving:

- Calories: 250
- Protein: 30g
- Carbohydrates: 10g
- Fat: 8g
- Sodium: 300mg
- Potassium: 600mg

Note: Adjust the seasonings and portion sizes according to your dietary needs.

VEGETABLE LASAGNA WITH WHOLE WHEAT NOODLES AND LOW-FAT CHEESE:

Preparation time: 30 minutes

Cooking time: 1 hour

Servings: 6

Ingredients:

- 9 whole wheat lasagna noodles
- 2 teaspoons olive oil
- 1 onion, chopped

- 2 cloves garlic, minced
- 1 zucchini, diced
- 1 yellow squash, diced
- 1 red bell pepper, diced
- 1 cup sliced mushrooms
- 2 cups low-sodium marinara sauce
- 1 teaspoon dried basil
- 1 teaspoon dried oregano
- 1/2 teaspoon salt
- 1/4 teaspoon black pepper
- 1 cup part-skim ricotta cheese
- 1 cup shredded low-fat mozzarella cheese
- 1/4 cup grated Parmesan cheese
- Chopped fresh basil for garnish

Directions:

- Preheat the oven to 375°F (190°C). Cook the lasagna noodles according to the package instructions. Drain and set aside.
- In a large skillet, heat the olive oil over medium heat. Add the chopped onion and minced garlic. Sauté for 2-3 minutes until the onion becomes translucent.
- Add the diced zucchini, yellow squash, red bell pepper, and sliced mushrooms to the skillet. Cook for 5-6 minutes until the vegetables are tender.

- Stir in the marinara sauce, dried basil, dried oregano, salt, and black pepper. Simmer for 5 minutes.
- In a small bowl, combine the ricotta cheese, shredded mozzarella cheese, and grated Parmesan cheese.
- Spread a thin layer of the vegetable sauce mixture in the bottom of a baking dish. Place 3 lasagna noodles on top.
- Spread half of the ricotta cheese mixture over the noodles. Top with half of the remaining vegetable sauce.
- Repeat the layering with the remaining 3 lasagna noodles, ricotta cheese mixture, and vegetable sauce.
- Cover the baking dish with foil and bake in the preheated oven for 40 minutes.
- Remove the foil and bake for an additional 10 minutes until the cheese is melted and bubbly.
- Let the lasagna cool for a few minutes before serving. Garnish with chopped fresh basil.

Nutritional information per serving:

- Calories: 350
- Protein: 18g
- Carbohydrates: 45g
- Fat: 10g
- Sodium: 400mg
- Potassium: 600mg

GRILLED PORK TENDERLOIN WITH ROASTED BRUSSELS SPROUTS AND SWEET POTATOES:

Preparation time: 15 minutes

Marinating time: 2 hours

Cooking time: 30 minutes

Servings: 4

Ingredients:

- 1 pound pork tenderloin
- 2 tablespoons low-sodium soy sauce
- 2 tablespoons balsamic vinegar
- 2 tablespoons olive oil
- 2 cloves garlic, minced
- 1 teaspoon dried rosemary
- 1 teaspoon dried thyme
- 1/2 teaspoon black pepper
- 1/2 teaspoon salt
- 1 pound Brussels sprouts, trimmed and halved
- 2 medium sweet potatoes, peeled and cubed
- 1 tablespoon olive oil

- Salt and pepper to taste

Directions:

- In a bowl, whisk together the soy sauce, balsamic vinegar, olive oil, minced garlic, dried rosemary, dried thyme, black pepper, and salt.
- Place the pork tenderloin in a resealable bag and pour the marinade over it. Seal the bag and refrigerate for at least 2 hours or overnight.
- Preheat the grill to medium-high heat.
- Remove the pork tenderloin from the marinade, discarding the excess marinade. Grill the tenderloin for about 15-20 minutes, turning occasionally, until it reaches an internal temperature of 145°F (63°C). Remove from the grill and let it rest for 5 minutes before slicing.
- Meanwhile, preheat the oven to 400°F (200°C). Place the halved Brussels sprouts and cubed sweet potatoes on a baking sheet. Drizzle with olive oil and sprinkle with salt and pepper. Toss to coat.
- Roast the Brussels sprouts and sweet potatoes in the preheated oven for 15-20 minutes until they are tender and slightly browned.
- Slice the grilled pork tenderloin and serve it with the roasted Brussels sprouts and sweet potatoes.

Nutritional information per serving:

- Calories: 300
- Protein: 25g
- Carbohydrates: 25g
- Fat: 10g
- Sodium: 300mg
- Potassium: 800mg

EGGPLANT PARMESAN WITH WHOLE GRAIN SPAGHETTI:

Preparation time: 30 minutes

Cooking time: 1 hour

Servings: 6

Ingredients:

- 1 large eggplant, sliced into 1/4-inch rounds
- 1/2 cup whole wheat flour
- 2 eggs, beaten
- 1 cup whole wheat bread crumbs
- 2 tablespoons grated Parmesan cheese
- 2 cups low-sodium marinara sauce

- 1 cup shredded mozzarella cheese
- 1/4 cup chopped fresh basil
- 12 ounces whole grain spaghetti
- Salt and pepper to taste

Directions:

- Preheat the oven to 375°F (190°C). Line a baking sheet with parchment paper.
- Place the whole wheat flour, beaten eggs, and whole wheat bread crumbs in three separate shallow dishes.
- Dip each eggplant slice in the flour, shaking off any excess. Then dip it into the beaten eggs, allowing any excess to drip off. Finally, coat it with the whole wheat bread crumbs, pressing gently to adhere. Place the coated eggplant slices on the prepared baking sheet.
- Bake the eggplant slices in the preheated oven for about 20 minutes, flipping halfway through, until they are golden brown and crispy.
- In a baking dish, spread a thin layer of marinara sauce. Arrange half of the baked eggplant slices over the sauce. Top the eggplant slices with another layer of marinara sauce, shredded mozzarella cheese, and chopped fresh basil.
- Repeat the layering with the remaining eggplant slices, marinara sauce, mozzarella cheese, and fresh basil.

- Cover the baking dish with foil and bake in the oven for 30 minutes.
- Meanwhile, cook the whole grain spaghetti according to the package instructions. Drain and toss with a little olive oil to prevent sticking.
- Remove the foil from the baking dish and bake for an additional 10 minutes until the cheese is melted and bubbly.
- Serve the eggplant Parmesan over whole grain spaghetti.

Nutritional information per serving:

- Calories: 350
- Protein: 15g
- Carbohydrates: 55g
- Fat: 10g
- Sodium: 400mg
- Potassium: 600mg

Note: Adjust the seasonings and portion sizes according to your dietary needs.

BAKED TERIYAKI CHICKEN THIGHS WITH CAULIFLOWER RICE:

Preparation time: 10 minutes

Marinating time: 1 hour

Cooking time: 35 minutes

Servings: 4

Ingredients:

- 4 bone-in, skin-on chicken thighs
- 1/4 cup low-sodium soy sauce
- 2 tablespoons honey
- 2 tablespoons rice vinegar
- 1 tablespoon grated fresh ginger
- 2 cloves garlic, minced
- 1 tablespoon cornstarch
- 2 tablespoons water
- 1 head cauliflower, cut into florets
- 2 tablespoons olive oil
- Salt and pepper to taste
- Sesame seeds for garnish
- Chopped green onions for garnish

Directions:

- In a bowl, whisk together the soy sauce, honey, rice vinegar, grated ginger, and minced garlic to make the teriyaki marinade.
- Place the chicken thighs in a resealable bag and pour the teriyaki marinade over them. Seal the bag and refrigerate for at least 1 hour or overnight.
- Preheat the oven to 400°F (200°C). Place the marinated chicken thighs in a baking dish, reserving the marinade.
- Bake the chicken thighs in the preheated oven for 30-35 minutes until they are cooked through and the skin is crispy.
- While the chicken is baking, prepare the cauliflower rice. Place the cauliflower florets in a food processor and pulse until they resemble rice grains.
- Heat the olive oil in a large skillet over medium heat. Add the cauliflower rice to the skillet and sauté for 5-6 minutes until it is tender.
- In a small bowl, whisk together the cornstarch and water to make a slurry.
- In a saucepan, pour the reserved teriyaki marinade and bring it to a simmer over medium heat. Stir in the cornstarch slurry and cook for 2-3 minutes until the sauce thickens.
- Remove the baked chicken thighs from the oven and brush them with the thickened teriyaki sauce. Sprinkle with sesame seeds and chopped green onions.
- Serve the baked teriyaki chicken thighs with cauliflower rice.

Nutritional information per serving:

- Calories: 350
- Protein: 25g
- Carbohydrates: 20g
- Fat: 20g
- Sodium: 450mg
- Potassium: 600mg

QUINOA AND BLACK BEAN SALAD WITH LIME DRESSING:

Preparation time: 15 minutes

Cooking time: 15 minutes

Servings: 4

Ingredients:

- 1 cup quinoa
- 2 cups water
- 1 can (15 ounces) black beans, rinsed and drained
- 1 red bell pepper, diced
- 1 cup corn kernels (fresh or frozen)
- 1/2 cup diced red onion

- 1/4 cup chopped fresh cilantro
- Juice of 2 limes
- 2 tablespoons olive oil
- 1 clove garlic, minced
- 1/2 teaspoon cumin
- Salt and pepper to taste
- Avocado slices for garnish (optional)

Directions:

- Rinse the quinoa under cold water. In a saucepan, bring the water to a boil. Add the rinsed quinoa and reduce the heat to low. Cover and simmer for 12-15 minutes until the quinoa is cooked and the water is absorbed. Remove from heat and let it cool.
- In a large bowl, combine the cooked quinoa, black beans, diced red bell pepper, corn kernels, diced red onion, and chopped cilantro.
- In a small bowl, whisk together the lime juice, olive oil, minced garlic, cumin, salt, and pepper to make the lime dressing.
- Pour the lime dressing over the quinoa and black bean mixture. Toss to combine and coat everything evenly.
- Garnish with avocado slices, if desired.
- Serve the quinoa and black bean salad chilled or at room temperature.

Nutritional information per serving:

- Calories: 300
- Protein: 12g
- Carbohydrates: 45g
- Fat: 8g
- Sodium: 200mg
- Potassium: 600mg

SPINACH AND MUSHROOM STUFFED CHICKEN BREAST WITH ROASTED CAULIFLOWER:

Preparation time: 15 minutes

Cooking time: 40 minutes

Servings: 4

Ingredients:

- 4 boneless, skinless chicken breasts
- 1 tablespoon olive oil
- 2 cloves garlic, minced
- 2 cups chopped spinach
- 1 cup sliced mushrooms
- 1/4 cup grated Parmesan cheese

- 1/4 cup shredded mozzarella cheese
- Salt and pepper to taste
- 1 head cauliflower, cut into florets
- 2 tablespoons olive oil
- Salt and pepper to taste

Directions:

- Preheat the oven to 375°F (190°C). Grease a baking dish.
- Using a sharp knife, cut a slit in the side of each chicken breast to create a pocket for stuffing.
- In a skillet, heat the olive oil over medium heat. Add the minced garlic and sauté for 1 minute until fragrant.
- Add the chopped spinach and sliced mushrooms to the skillet. Cook for 3-4 minutes until the vegetables are wilted and any excess moisture has evaporated.
- Remove the skillet from heat and stir in the grated Parmesan cheese and shredded mozzarella cheese. Season with salt and pepper to taste.
- Stuff each chicken breast with the spinach and mushroom mixture. Secure with toothpicks if necessary.
- Place the stuffed chicken breasts in the prepared baking dish. Bake in the preheated oven for 25-30 minutes until the chicken is cooked through and no longer pink in the center.

- While the chicken is baking, prepare the roasted cauliflower. Place the cauliflower florets on a baking sheet. Drizzle with olive oil and sprinkle with salt and pepper. Toss to coat.
- Roast the cauliflower in the preheated oven for 15-20 minutes until it is tender and lightly browned.
- Remove the toothpicks from the chicken breasts before serving. Serve the spinach and mushroom stuffed chicken breasts with roasted cauliflower.

Nutritional information per serving:

- Calories: 300
- Protein: 40g
- Carbohydrates: 10g
- Fat: 12g
- Sodium: 400mg
- Potassium: 900mg

Note: Adjust the seasonings and portion sizes according to your dietary needs.

BAKED ZUCCHINI BOATS FILLED WITH GROUND TURKEY AND TOMATO SAUCE:

Preparation time: 15 minutes

Cooking time: 40 minutes

Servings: 4

Ingredients:

- 4 medium zucchini
- 1 tablespoon olive oil
- 1/2 cup diced onion
- 2 cloves garlic, minced
- 1 pound lean ground turkey
- 1 cup low-sodium tomato sauce
- 1 teaspoon dried oregano
- 1/2 teaspoon dried basil
- 1/4 teaspoon red pepper flakes (optional)
- Salt and pepper to taste
- 1/4 cup grated Parmesan cheese
- Fresh parsley for garnish

Directions:

- Preheat the oven to 375°F (190°C). Grease a baking dish.
- Cut each zucchini in half lengthwise. Use a spoon to scoop out the center of each zucchini half, creating a hollow "boat." Reserve the scooped-out zucchini flesh.

- Heat the olive oil in a skillet over medium heat. Add the diced onion and minced garlic. Sauté for 2-3 minutes until the onion is translucent and fragrant.
- Add the ground turkey to the skillet and cook until it is browned and cooked through. Drain any excess fat if necessary.
- Chop the reserved zucchini flesh and add it to the skillet with the cooked ground turkey. Cook for an additional 2-3 minutes until the zucchini is tender.
- Stir in the tomato sauce, dried oregano, dried basil, red pepper flakes (if using), salt, and pepper. Simmer the mixture for 5 minutes to allow the flavors to meld together.
- Place the zucchini boats in the prepared baking dish. Spoon the ground turkey mixture into each boat, dividing it evenly.
- Sprinkle the grated Parmesan cheese over the filled zucchini boats.
- Bake in the preheated oven for 25-30 minutes until the zucchini is tender and the filling is heated through.
- Garnish with fresh parsley before serving.

Nutritional information per serving:

- Calories: 250
- Protein: 25g
- Carbohydrates: 10g
- Fat: 12g

- Sodium: 400mg
- Potassium: 600mg

GRILLED STEAK WITH PORTOBELLO MUSHROOMS AND ROASTED GREEN BEANS:

Preparation time: 15 minutes

Marinating time: 30 minutes

Cooking time: 20 minutes

Servings: 4

Ingredients:

- 4 beef steaks (such as sirloin or ribeye), about 6 ounces each
- 1/4 cup low-sodium soy sauce
- 2 tablespoons balsamic vinegar
- 2 cloves garlic, minced
- 1 teaspoon dried rosemary
- 4 large portobello mushrooms
- 1 pound green beans, trimmed
- 2 tablespoons olive oil
- Salt and pepper to taste

Directions:

- In a shallow dish, whisk together the soy sauce, balsamic vinegar, minced garlic, and dried rosemary to make the marinade.
- Place the steaks in the marinade and turn to coat them evenly. Let the steaks marinate at room temperature for 30 minutes.
- Preheat the grill to medium-high heat.
- Remove the steaks from the marinade, allowing any excess marinade to drip off. Season the steaks with salt and pepper.
- Grill the steaks for about 4-5 minutes per side for medium-rare, or adjust the cooking time according to your desired doneness. Remove the steaks from the grill and let them rest for a few minutes before slicing.
- While the steaks are grilling, prepare the portobello mushrooms. Remove the stems and gently scrape out the gills using a spoon.
- In a bowl, toss the portobello mushrooms and green beans with olive oil, salt, and pepper.
- Place the mushrooms and green beans on a baking sheet. Roast in the oven at 400°F (200°C) for 15-20 minutes until the mushrooms are tender and the green beans are crisp-tender.
- Serve the grilled steaks with portobello mushrooms and roasted green beans.

Nutritional information per serving:

- Calories: 400
- Protein: 40g
- Carbohydrates: 10g
- Fat: 20g
- Sodium: 450mg
- Potassium: 900mg

MOROCCAN CHICKPEA STEW WITH COUSCOUS:

Preparation time: 15 minutes

Cooking time: 30 minutes

Servings: 4

Ingredients:

- 1 tablespoon olive oil
- 1 onion, diced
- 2 cloves garlic, minced
- 2 carrots, diced
- 2 teaspoons ground cumin
- 1 teaspoon ground coriander
- 1 teaspoon ground turmeric
- 1/2 teaspoon ground cinnamon

- 1/4 teaspoon cayenne pepper (optional)
- 1 can (15 ounces) diced tomatoes
- 2 cups low-sodium vegetable broth
- 2 cans (15 ounces each) chickpeas, rinsed and drained
- 1 cup diced zucchini
- 1 cup diced red bell pepper
- 1/4 cup chopped fresh parsley
- Salt and pepper to taste
- 1 cup whole wheat couscous
- Chopped fresh cilantro for garnish

Directions:

- In a large pot, heat the olive oil over medium heat. Add the diced onion and minced garlic. Sauté for 2-3 minutes until the onion is translucent and fragrant.
- Add the diced carrots to the pot and cook for 3-4 minutes until they begin to soften.
- Stir in the ground cumin, ground coriander, ground turmeric, ground cinnamon, and cayenne pepper (if using). Cook for 1 minute to toast the spices and release their flavors.
- Add the diced tomatoes (including the juice) and vegetable broth to the pot. Bring the mixture to a boil.
- Reduce the heat to low and add the rinsed and drained chickpeas, diced zucchini, diced red bell pepper, and chopped fresh parsley

to the pot. Simmer for 15-20 minutes until the vegetables are tender and the flavors have melded together. Season with salt and pepper to taste.

- While the stew is simmering, prepare the whole wheat couscous according to the package instructions.
- Fluff the cooked couscous with a fork.
- Serve the Moroccan chickpea stew over the whole wheat couscous. Garnish with chopped fresh cilantro.

Nutritional information per serving:

- Calories: 400
- Protein: 15g
- Carbohydrates: 70g
- Fat: 8g
- Sodium: 400mg
- Potassium: 800mg

Note: Adjust the seasonings and portion sizes according to your dietary needs.

BAKED EGGPLANT ROLLATINI WITH RICOTTA AND MARINARA SAUCE:

Preparation time: 30 minutes

Cooking time: 45 minutes

Servings: 4

Ingredients:

- 2 large eggplants
- Olive oil for brushing
- Salt and pepper to taste
- 1 cup low-sodium marinara sauce
- 1 cup low-fat ricotta cheese
- 1/2 cup grated Parmesan cheese
- 1/4 cup chopped fresh basil
- 1/4 cup chopped fresh parsley
- 1/2 teaspoon dried oregano
- 1/2 teaspoon garlic powder
- 1/4 teaspoon red pepper flakes (optional)

Directions:

- Preheat the oven to 375°F (190°C). Grease a baking dish.
- Slice the eggplants lengthwise into 1/4-inch thick slices.
- Place the eggplant slices on a baking sheet. Brush both sides of the slices with olive oil and season with salt and pepper.

- Bake the eggplant slices in the preheated oven for 10-12 minutes until they are tender and slightly browned.
- In a bowl, combine the ricotta cheese, grated Parmesan cheese, chopped fresh basil, chopped fresh parsley, dried oregano, garlic powder, and red pepper flakes (if using). Mix well.
- Spread a thin layer of marinara sauce on the bottom of the greased baking dish.
- Take one eggplant slice and spread a spoonful of the ricotta mixture on top. Roll up the eggplant slice and place it seam side down in the baking dish. Repeat with the remaining eggplant slices and ricotta mixture.
- Pour the remaining marinara sauce over the rolled eggplant slices in the baking dish.
- Cover the baking dish with foil and bake in the preheated oven for 25-30 minutes until the sauce is bubbly and the cheese is melted.
- Remove the foil and bake for an additional 5 minutes until the top is golden brown.
- Serve the baked eggplant rollatini with a side of whole grain spaghetti or a green salad.

Nutritional information per serving:

- Calories: 250
- Protein: 12g

- Carbohydrates: 30g
- Fat: 8g
- Sodium: 400mg
- Potassium: 800mg

GRILLED VEGETABLE SKEWERS WITH BALSAMIC GLAZE SERVED WITH WILD RICE:

Preparation time: 20 minutes

Cooking time: 15 minutes

Servings: 4

Ingredients:

- 2 small zucchini, cut into thick slices
- 1 red bell pepper, cut into chunks
- 1 yellow bell pepper, cut into chunks
- 1 red onion, cut into wedges
- 8 cherry tomatoes
- 1 tablespoon olive oil
- Salt and pepper to taste
- 1/4 cup balsamic vinegar
- 2 tablespoons honey or maple syrup

- 2 cups cooked wild rice
- Fresh parsley for garnish

Directions:

- Preheat the grill to medium-high heat.
- Thread the zucchini slices, bell pepper chunks, red onion wedges, and cherry tomatoes onto skewers. Brush the vegetables with olive oil and season with salt and pepper.
- In a small saucepan, combine the balsamic vinegar and honey (or maple syrup). Bring the mixture to a simmer over medium heat. Cook for 3-4 minutes until the glaze has thickened slightly. Remove from heat.
- Place the vegetable skewers on the preheated grill. Grill for 10-12 minutes, turning occasionally, until the vegetables are tender and lightly charred.
- Brush the grilled vegetable skewers with the balsamic glaze, reserving some for serving.
- Serve the grilled vegetable skewers over cooked wild rice. Drizzle with the remaining balsamic glaze and garnish with fresh parsley.

Nutritional information per serving:

- Calories: 200
- Protein: 4g

- Carbohydrates: 40g
- Fat: 4g
- Sodium: 50mg
- Potassium: 450mg

DR. HERMIONE MENDEZ

VEGAN
DIABETIC RENAL
DIET COOKBOOK

100+

diabetes and
kidney-friendly
100% VEGAN meals

**14-DAY
MEAL PLAN**

GET ON AMAZON TODAY!

CHAPTER 6: KIDNEY-FRIENDLY SNACKS AND SIDES:

BAKED SWEET POTATO FRIES WITH HERBS:

Time: 40 minutes

Servings: 4

Ingredients:

- 2 large sweet potatoes, peeled and cut into fries
- 1 tablespoon olive oil
- 1 teaspoon dried herbs (such as thyme, rosemary, or oregano)
- Salt substitute (low-sodium) and black pepper to taste

Directions:

- Preheat the oven to 425°F (220°C).
- In a large bowl, toss the sweet potato fries with olive oil, dried herbs, salt substitute, and black pepper until well coated.
- Spread the fries in a single layer on a baking sheet.

- Bake for about 30 minutes, or until the fries are crispy and golden brown.
- Serve hot.

Nutritional Information (per serving):

- Calories: 120
- Protein: 2g
- Carbohydrates: 22g
- Fat: 3g
- Sodium: 10mg
- Potassium: 250mg

CUCUMBER AND TOMATO SALAD WITH LEMON DRESSING:

Time: 15 minutes

Servings: 4

Ingredients:

- 2 cucumbers, sliced
- 2 tomatoes, diced
- 1 small red onion, thinly sliced
- 2 tablespoons fresh lemon juice

- 1 tablespoon olive oil
- 1 teaspoon dried dill
- Salt substitute and black pepper to taste

Directions:

- In a large bowl, combine the cucumbers, tomatoes, and red onion.
- In a small bowl, whisk together the lemon juice, olive oil, dried dill, salt substitute, and black pepper.
- Pour the dressing over the cucumber and tomato mixture, and toss gently to combine.
- Refrigerate for at least 30 minutes before serving to allow the flavors to meld.

Nutritional Information (per serving):

- Calories: 60
- Protein: 1g
- Carbohydrates: 8g
- Fat: 3g
- Sodium: 5mg
- Potassium: 200mg

ROASTED BEET CHIPS:

Time: 45 minutes

Servings: 4

Ingredients:

- 4 medium beets, peeled and thinly sliced
- 1 tablespoon olive oil
- Salt substitute and black pepper to taste

Directions:

- Preheat the oven to 350°F (175°C).
- In a large bowl, toss the beet slices with olive oil, salt substitute, and black pepper until well coated.
- Arrange the beet slices in a single layer on a baking sheet.
- Bake for about 30-35 minutes, or until the chips are crisp and slightly browned.
- Allow the chips to cool before serving.

Nutritional Information (per serving):

- Calories: 70
- Protein: 2g
- Carbohydrates: 12g
- Fat: 2g
- Sodium: 10mg

- Potassium: 350mg

ZUCCHINI AND CARROT MUFFINS (LOW-SODIUM):

Time: 45 minutes

Servings: 12 muffins

Ingredients:

- 1 cup grated zucchini
- 1 cup grated carrot
- 2 cups all-purpose flour
- 1/2 cup granulated sugar
- 2 teaspoons baking powder (low-sodium)
- 1/2 teaspoon baking soda
- 1/2 teaspoon ground cinnamon
- 1/4 teaspoon salt substitute
- 2 large eggs
- 1/2 cup unsalted butter, melted
- 1/2 cup milk

Directions:

- Preheat the oven to 375°F (190°C). Grease a muffin tin or line it with paper liners.

- In a large bowl, combine the grated zucchini, grated carrot, flour, sugar, baking powder, baking soda, cinnamon, and salt substitute.
- In a separate bowl, whisk together the eggs, melted butter, and milk.
- Pour the wet ingredients into the dry ingredients and stir until just combined.
- Spoon the batter into the prepared muffin tin, filling each cup about two-thirds full.
- Bake for 20-25 minutes, or until a toothpick inserted into the center of a muffin comes out clean.
- Allow the muffins to cool for a few minutes before transferring them to a wire rack to cool completely.

Nutritional Information (per serving - 1 muffin):

- Calories: 180
- Protein: 4g
- Carbohydrates: 22g
- Fat: 8g
- Sodium: 40mg
- Potassium: 120mg

EDAMAME HUMMUS WITH RAW VEGETABLES:

Time: 10 minutes

Servings: 6

Ingredients:

- 1 cup shelled edamame, cooked and cooled
- 2 tablespoons tahini (low-sodium)
- 2 tablespoons fresh lemon juice
- 2 tablespoons olive oil
- 1 clove garlic, minced
- Salt substitute and black pepper to taste
- Raw vegetables (such as carrot sticks, cucumber slices, and bell pepper strips), for serving

Directions:

- In a food processor, combine the edamame, tahini, lemon juice, olive oil, garlic, salt substitute, and black pepper.
- Process until smooth and creamy, scraping down the sides as needed.
- Transfer the edamame hummus to a serving bowl.
- Serve with raw vegetables for dipping.

Nutritional Information (per serving):

- Calories: 100

- Protein: 5g
- Carbohydrates: 5g
- Fat: 7g
- Sodium: 15mg
- Potassium: 150mg

(Note: Continued in the next message due to character limit)

ROASTED CHICKPEAS WITH SPICES:

Time: 40 minutes

Servings: 4

Ingredients:

- 2 cups cooked chickpeas (low-sodium)
- 1 tablespoon olive oil
- 1 teaspoon ground cumin
- 1/2 teaspoon paprika
- 1/4 teaspoon garlic powder
- Salt substitute and black pepper to taste

Directions:

- Preheat the oven to 400°F (200°C).

- In a bowl, toss the cooked chickpeas with olive oil, cumin, paprika, garlic powder, salt substitute, and black pepper until well coated.
- Spread the chickpeas in a single layer on a baking sheet.
- Roast for 30-35 minutes, stirring occasionally, until the chickpeas are crispy and golden.
- Remove from the oven and let them cool before serving.

Nutritional Information (per serving):

- Calories: 150
- Protein: 7g
- Carbohydrates: 20g
- Fat: 5g
- Sodium: 10mg
- Potassium: 200mg

BAKED PARMESAN ZUCCHINI ROUNDS:

Time: 30 minutes

Servings: 4

Ingredients:

- 2 zucchini, sliced into rounds

- 1/4 cup grated Parmesan cheese (low-sodium)
- 1/4 teaspoon dried thyme
- 1/4 teaspoon dried oregano
- Salt substitute and black pepper to taste
- Cooking spray

Directions:

- Preheat the oven to 425°F (220°C). Line a baking sheet with parchment paper and lightly coat it with cooking spray.
- In a small bowl, combine the grated Parmesan cheese, dried thyme, dried oregano, salt substitute, and black pepper.
- Place the zucchini rounds on the prepared baking sheet. Sprinkle the Parmesan mixture evenly over the zucchini.
- Bake for 15-20 minutes, or until the zucchini is tender and the Parmesan is melted and golden.
- Remove from the oven and let them cool slightly before serving.

Nutritional Information (per serving):

- Calories: 80
- Protein: 6g
- Carbohydrates: 7g
- Fat: 4g
- Sodium: 50mg
- Potassium: 300mg

QUINOA AND BLACK BEAN SALAD:

Time: 25 minutes

Servings: 4

Ingredients:

- 1 cup cooked quinoa
- 1 cup canned black beans (low-sodium), rinsed and drained
- 1 cup cherry tomatoes, halved
- 1/2 cup diced red bell pepper
- 1/4 cup chopped fresh cilantro
- 2 tablespoons fresh lime juice
- 1 tablespoon olive oil
- 1/2 teaspoon ground cumin
- Salt substitute and black pepper to taste

Directions:

- In a large bowl, combine the cooked quinoa, black beans, cherry tomatoes, diced red bell pepper, and chopped cilantro.
- In a separate small bowl, whisk together the lime juice, olive oil, ground cumin, salt substitute, and black pepper.

- Pour the dressing over the quinoa and black bean mixture. Toss gently to combine.
- Refrigerate for at least 15 minutes to allow the flavors to blend before serving.

Nutritional Information (per serving):

- Calories: 180
- Protein: 7g
- Carbohydrates: 27g
- Fat: 5g
- Sodium: 10mg
- Potassium: 250mg

FRESH FRUIT SKEWERS WITH YOGURT DIP:

Time: 15 minutes

Servings: 4

Ingredients:

- Assorted fresh fruits (such as strawberries, pineapple chunks, melon cubes, and grapes)
- 1 cup plain Greek yogurt (low-sodium)
- 1 tablespoon honey

- 1/2 teaspoon vanilla extract

Directions:

- Thread the assorted fresh fruits onto skewers.
- In a small bowl, whisk together the Greek yogurt, honey, and vanilla extract until smooth.
- Serve the fresh fruit skewers with the yogurt dip on the side.

Nutritional Information (per serving):

- Calories: 120
- Protein: 8g
- Carbohydrates: 22g
- Fat: 0g
- Sodium: 40mg
- Potassium: 250mg

CABBAGE AND CARROT SLAW WITH LOW-SODIUM DRESSING:

Time: 20 minutes

Servings: 4

Ingredients:

- 2 cups shredded green cabbage
- 1 cup shredded carrots
- 2 green onions, thinly sliced
- 1/4 cup chopped fresh parsley
- 2 tablespoons apple cider vinegar (low-sodium)
- 1 tablespoon olive oil
- 1 teaspoon Dijon mustard
- Salt substitute and black pepper to taste

Directions:

- In a large bowl, combine the shredded cabbage, shredded carrots, sliced green onions, and chopped parsley.
- In a small bowl, whisk together the apple cider vinegar, olive oil, Dijon mustard, salt substitute, and black pepper.
- Pour the dressing over the cabbage and carrot mixture. Toss well to coat.
- Refrigerate for at least 10 minutes before serving to allow the flavors to meld.

Nutritional Information (per serving):

- Calories: 60
- Protein: 1g
- Carbohydrates: 8g
- Fat: 3g

- Sodium: 15mg
- Potassium: 200mg

CHAPTER 7: DELECTABLE DESSERTS FOR CKD:

BERRY AND GREEK YOGURT POPSICLES (LOW-SUGAR):

Time: 10 minutes (plus freezing time)

Servings: 6 popsicles

Ingredients:

- 1 cup mixed berries (such as strawberries, blueberries, and raspberries), fresh or frozen
- 2 cups low-sugar Greek yogurt
- 2 tablespoons honey (optional, adjust to taste)

Directions:

- In a blender, puree the mixed berries until smooth.
- In a bowl, combine the Greek yogurt and honey (if using), and mix well.
- Layer the berry puree and Greek yogurt in popsicle molds, alternating between the two.

- Insert popsicle sticks into the molds and freeze for at least 4 hours or until firm.
- To remove the popsicles from the molds, run them under warm water for a few seconds and gently pull them out.
- Enjoy these refreshing low-sugar popsicles!

Nutritional Information (per serving):

- Calories: 90
- Protein: 6g
- Carbohydrates: 14g
- Fat: 1g
- Sodium: 30mg
- Potassium: 80mg

BAKED APPLE SLICES WITH CINNAMON AND ALMOND BUTTER:

Time: 25 minutes

Servings: 2

Ingredients:

- 2 apples, cored and sliced
- 1 teaspoon cinnamon

- 2 tablespoons low-sodium almond butter

Directions:

- Preheat the oven to 350°F (175°C) and line a baking sheet with parchment paper.
- In a bowl, toss the apple slices with cinnamon until coated.
- Arrange the apple slices on the baking sheet in a single layer.
- Bake for 20 minutes or until the apples are tender.
- Serve the baked apple slices warm, topped with a tablespoon of low-sodium almond butter.

Nutritional Information (per serving):

- Calories: 120
- Protein: 3g
- Carbohydrates: 20g
- Fat: 4g
- Sodium: 20mg
- Potassium: 150mg

COCONUT MILK RICE PUDDING WITH CARDAMOM:

Time: 40 minutes

Servings: 4

Ingredients:

- 1 cup white rice
- 2 cups unsweetened coconut milk
- 2 cups water
- 1/4 cup low-sugar sweetener (such as stevia or erythritol)
- 1/2 teaspoon ground cardamom
- 2 tablespoons unsweetened shredded coconut (optional, for garnish)

Directions:

- Rinse the rice under cold water until the water runs clear.
- In a saucepan, combine the rinsed rice, coconut milk, water, low-sugar sweetener, and ground cardamom.
- Bring the mixture to a boil over medium heat, then reduce the heat to low and simmer for 30 minutes, stirring occasionally.
- Once the rice is cooked and the pudding has thickened, remove from heat and let it cool slightly.
- Divide the rice pudding into serving bowls and sprinkle with unsweetened shredded coconut if desired.
- Serve warm or chilled.

Nutritional Information (per serving):

- Calories: 230

- Protein: 3g
- Carbohydrates: 38g
- Fat: 8g
- Sodium: 10mg
- Potassium: 70mg

LEMON POPPY SEED MUFFINS (LOW-PHOSPHORUS):

Time: 35 minutes

Servings: 12 muffins

Ingredients:

- 2 cups all-purpose flour
- 1/2 cup low-phosphorus baking powder
- 1/4 teaspoon salt
- 1/2 cup unsalted butter, softened
- 1 cup low-sugar sweetener (such as stevia or erythritol)
- 2 large eggs
- 1 cup low-fat milk
- Zest of 2 lemons
- Juice of 1 lemon
- 1 tablespoon poppy seeds

Directions:

- Preheat the oven to 375°F (190°C) and line a muffin tin with paper liners.
- In a bowl, whisk together the flour, low-phosphorus baking powder, and salt.
- In a separate bowl, cream together the softened butter and low-sugar sweetener until light and fluffy.
- Add the eggs one at a time, beating well after each addition.
- Stir in the milk, lemon zest, lemon juice, and poppy seeds.
- Gradually add the dry ingredients to the wet ingredients, mixing until just combined.
- Spoon the batter into the prepared muffin tin, filling each cup about 2/3 full.
- Bake for 18-20 minutes or until a toothpick inserted into the center comes out clean.
- Allow the muffins to cool in the tin for a few minutes before transferring them to a wire rack to cool completely.

Nutritional Information (per serving/muffin):

- Calories: 170
- Protein: 4g
- Carbohydrates: 25g
- Fat: 7g

- Sodium: 50mg
- Potassium: 90mg

MANGO SORBET (LOW-POTASSIUM):

Time: 15 minutes (plus freezing time)

Servings: 4

Ingredients:

- 2 ripe mangoes, peeled and pitted
- 1/4 cup low-sugar sweetener (such as stevia or erythritol)
- Juice of 1 lime
- Fresh mint leaves, for garnish (optional)

Directions:

- Cut the mango flesh into chunks and place them in a blender or food processor.
- Add the low-sugar sweetener and lime juice to the blender.
- Blend until smooth and creamy.
- Pour the mixture into a shallow dish and freeze for at least 4 hours or until firm.

- Every 30 minutes during the freezing process, remove the dish from the freezer and stir the sorbet to prevent ice crystals from forming.
- Once fully frozen, scoop the mango sorbet into bowls or glasses.
- Garnish with fresh mint leaves if desired.
- Serve and enjoy!

Nutritional Information (per serving):

- Calories: 90
- Protein: 1g
- Carbohydrates: 23g
- Fat: 0g
- Sodium: 0mg
- Potassium: 150mg

DARK CHOCOLATE AND ALMOND BARK (LOW-SUGAR):

Time: 15 minutes (plus chilling time)

Servings: 8

Ingredients:

- 8 ounces dark chocolate (at least 70% cocoa), chopped

- 1/2 cup unsalted almonds, chopped
- 1 tablespoon low-sugar sweetener (such as stevia or erythritol)

Directions:

- Line a baking sheet with parchment paper.
- In a heatproof bowl set over a saucepan of simmering water, melt the dark chocolate, stirring occasionally until smooth.
- Remove the bowl from heat and stir in the chopped almonds and low-sugar sweetener.
- Pour the mixture onto the prepared baking sheet and spread it into a thin layer.
- Place the baking sheet in the refrigerator and chill for about 1 hour or until the chocolate is firm.
- Once chilled, break the bark into pieces and store in an airtight container in the refrigerator.

Nutritional Information (per serving):

- Calories: 150
- Protein: 3g
- Carbohydrates: 10g
- Fat: 12g
- Sodium: 0mg
- Potassium: 100mg

GREEK YOGURT CHEESECAKE BITES WITH FRESH BERRIES:

Time: 30 minutes (plus chilling time)

Servings: 12 bites

Ingredients:

- 1 cup low-fat cream cheese
- 1/2 cup low-fat Greek yogurt
- 1/4 cup low-sugar sweetener (such as stevia or erythritol)
- 1 teaspoon vanilla extract
- Fresh berries (such as strawberries, blueberries, and raspberries), for topping

Directions:

- In a bowl, combine the low-fat cream cheese, low-fat Greek yogurt, low-sugar sweetener, and vanilla extract.
- Beat the mixture until smooth and well combined.
- Spoon the mixture into a mini muffin tin or silicone mold, filling each cavity about 2/3 full.
- Smooth the tops with a spatula and tap the mold gently on the counter to remove any air bubbles.

- Refrigerate the cheesecake bites for at least 2 hours or until firm.
- Once chilled, remove the cheesecake bites from the mold and top each one with fresh berries.
- Serve and enjoy these delightful treats!

Nutritional Information (per serving/bite):

- Calories: 60
- Protein: 3g
- Carbohydrates: 5g
- Fat: 3g
- Sodium: 60mg
- Potassium: 50mg

VANILLA CHIA PUDDING WITH SLICED PEACHES:

Time: 5 minutes (plus chilling time)

Servings: 2

Ingredients:

- 1 cup unsweetened almond milk
- 1/4 cup chia seeds
- 1 tablespoon low-sugar sweetener (such as stevia or erythritol)
- 1 teaspoon vanilla extract

- 2 ripe peaches, sliced

Directions:

- In a bowl, whisk together the almond milk, chia seeds, low-sugar sweetener, and vanilla extract.
- Let the mixture sit for 5 minutes, then whisk again to prevent clumping.
- Cover the bowl and refrigerate for at least 2 hours or overnight until the chia pudding thickens.
- Stir the pudding before serving to break up any clumps.
- Divide the chia pudding into serving bowls and top with sliced peaches.
- Enjoy this delicious and nutritious pudding!

Nutritional Information (per serving):

- Calories: 150
- Protein: 4g
- Carbohydrates: 17g
- Fat: 8g
- Sodium: 40mg
- Potassium: 200mg

CINNAMON BAKED PEARS WITH GREEK YOGURT:

Time: 35 minutes

Servings: 4

Ingredients:

- 4 ripe pears, halved and cored
- 1 tablespoon low-sugar sweetener (such as stevia or erythritol)
- 1 teaspoon ground cinnamon
- 1 cup low-fat Greek yogurt
- 2 tablespoons chopped walnuts (optional, for garnish)

Directions:

- Preheat the oven to 375°F (190°C) and line a baking dish with parchment paper.
- Place the pear halves, cut side up, in the baking dish.
- In a small bowl, mix together the low-sugar sweetener and ground cinnamon.
- Sprinkle the cinnamon mixture evenly over the pear halves.
- Bake for 25-30 minutes or until the pears are tender.
- Remove from the oven and let them cool slightly.
- Serve the baked pears with a dollop of low-fat Greek yogurt and sprinkle with chopped walnuts if desired.

Nutritional Information (per serving):

- Calories: 130
- Protein: 6g
- Carbohydrates: 25g
- Fat: 2g
- Sodium: 20mg
- Potassium: 200mg

PUMPKIN SPICE ENERGY BALLS (LOW-PHOSPHORUS):

Time: 15 minutes

Servings: 12 balls

Ingredients:

- 1 cup unsalted pumpkin seeds
- 1 cup pitted dates
- 2 tablespoons unsweetened pumpkin puree
- 1 teaspoon pumpkin pie spice
- 1/4 cup unsweetened shredded coconut (for rolling, optional)

Directions:

- Place the pumpkin seeds in a food processor and pulse until finely ground.

- Add the pitted dates, pumpkin puree, and pumpkin pie spice to the food processor.
- Process until the mixture forms a sticky dough.
- Scoop out tablespoon-sized portions of the dough and roll them into balls.
- If desired, roll the energy balls in unsweetened shredded coconut to coat.
- Place the energy balls in an airtight container and refrigerate for at least 1 hour to firm up.
- Enjoy these tasty and nutritious energy balls as a snack!

Nutritional Information (per serving/ball):

- Calories: 120
- Protein: 4g
- Carbohydrates: 12g
- Fat: 7g
- Sodium: 0mg
- Potassium: 120mg

CHAPTER 8: BEVERAGES FOR KIDNEY HEALTH:

LEMON WATER WITH FRESH MINT

Time: 5 minutes

Servings: 1

Ingredients:

- 1 cup water
- 1/2 lemon, juiced
- Few sprigs of fresh mint leaves
- Ice cubes (optional)

Directions:

- In a glass, combine water and freshly squeezed lemon juice.
- Add fresh mint leaves to the glass.
- Optionally, add ice cubes to chill the drink.
- Stir well and let it sit for a few minutes to allow the flavors to infuse.
- Enjoy the refreshing lemon water with a hint of mint.

Nutritional Information:

- Calories: 5 kcal
- Sodium: 0 mg
- Potassium: 45 mg

CRANBERRY JUICE (UNSWEETENED, LOW-SUGAR)

Time: 10 minutes

Servings: 2

Ingredients:

- 1 cup unsweetened cranberry juice
- 1 cup water
- 1/2 lemon, juiced
- Ice cubes (optional)

Directions:

- In a pitcher, combine unsweetened cranberry juice, water, and freshly squeezed lemon juice.
- Stir well to mix all the ingredients.
- Optionally, add ice cubes to chill the juice.
- Serve the cranberry juice in glasses.

- Enjoy the tart and refreshing cranberry juice.

Nutritional Information:

- Calories: 20 kcal
- Sodium: 2 mg
- Potassium: 30 mg

CUCUMBER AND MINT INFUSED WATER

Time: 5 minutes

Servings: 1

Ingredients:

- 1 cup water
- 1/4 cucumber, thinly sliced
- Few sprigs of fresh mint leaves
- Ice cubes (optional)

Directions:

- In a glass or pitcher, combine water, sliced cucumber, and fresh mint leaves.
- Stir gently to distribute the flavors.
- Optionally, add ice cubes to chill the infused water.

- Let it sit for a few minutes to allow the flavors to infuse.
- Serve the cucumber and mint infused water in a glass.
- Enjoy the refreshing and hydrating drink.

Nutritional Information:

- Calories: 5 kcal
- Sodium: 1 mg
- Potassium: 45 mg

HERBAL TEA (NETTLE, DANDELION, OR GINGER)

Time: Varies (follow package instructions)

Servings: 1

Ingredients:

- 1 herbal tea bag (nettle, dandelion, or ginger)
- 1 cup hot water
- Lemon or lime wedges (optional)
- Sugar substitute (optional)

Directions:

- Place the herbal tea bag in a cup.
- Pour hot water over the tea bag.

- Let it steep for the recommended time mentioned on the tea bag package.
- Remove the tea bag and discard.
- Optionally, add lemon or lime wedges for extra flavor.
- If desired, sweeten the tea with a sugar substitute.
- Stir well and enjoy the soothing herbal tea.

Nutritional Information:

- Calories: 0 kcal
- Sodium: 0 mg
- Potassium: 0 mg

WATERMELON LIME COOLER (LOW-POTASSIUM)

Time: 10 minutes

Servings: 2

Ingredients:

- 2 cups seedless watermelon, diced
- Juice of 1 lime
- Ice cubes (optional)
- Fresh mint leaves for garnish (optional)

Directions:

- In a blender, add the diced watermelon and lime juice.
- Blend until smooth and well combined.
- Optionally, add ice cubes to chill the drink.
- Pour the watermelon lime cooler into glasses.
- Garnish with fresh mint leaves, if desired.
- Serve and enjoy the refreshing watermelon lime cooler.

Nutritional Information:

- Calories: 45 kcal
- Sodium: 2 mg
- Potassium: 100 mg

HIBISCUS ICED TEA (NATURALLY LOW IN POTASSIUM)

Time: 15 minutes (plus chilling time)

Servings: 4

Ingredients:

- 4 cups water
- 4 hibiscus tea bags
- Sugar substitute (optional)

- Ice cubes (optional)
- Lemon slices for garnish (optional)

Directions:

- Bring the water to a boil in a saucepan.
- Remove from heat and add the hibiscus tea bags.
- Let the tea steep for about 10 minutes.
- Remove the tea bags and discard.
- If desired, sweeten the tea with a sugar substitute.
- Allow the tea to cool to room temperature.
- Transfer the tea to a pitcher and refrigerate until chilled.
- Serve the hibiscus iced tea in glasses over ice cubes, if desired.
- Garnish with lemon slices, if desired.
- Enjoy the vibrant and refreshing hibiscus iced tea.

Nutritional Information:

- Calories: 0 kcal
- Sodium: 0 mg
- Potassium: 0 mg

HOMEMADE ELECTROLYTE DRINK WITH COCONUT WATER AND LIME

Time: 5 minutes

Servings: 1

Ingredients:

- 1 cup coconut water (low-potassium)
- Juice of 1 lime
- 1/8 teaspoon salt substitute (low-sodium)
- 1 teaspoon sugar substitute

Directions:

- In a glass, combine coconut water, lime juice, salt substitute, and sugar substitute.
- Stir well until the salt substitute and sugar substitute are dissolved.
- Chill the electrolyte drink in the refrigerator if desired.
- Serve the homemade electrolyte drink and rehydrate yourself.

Nutritional Information:

- Calories: 30 kcal
- Sodium: 60 mg
- Potassium: 240 mg

GINGER TURMERIC GOLDEN MILK (LOW-PHOSPHORUS)

Time: 10 minutes

Servings: 1

Ingredients:

- 1 cup unsweetened almond milk (low-phosphorus)
- 1/2 teaspoon ground turmeric
- 1/4 teaspoon ground ginger
- 1/8 teaspoon ground cinnamon
- Pinch of black pepper
- 1 teaspoon honey or sugar substitute

Directions:

- In a small saucepan, heat the almond milk over medium heat until warm (do not boil).
- Add the ground turmeric, ground ginger, ground cinnamon, and black pepper to the warm almond milk.
- Whisk the mixture well until the spices are fully incorporated.
- Stir in honey or a sugar substitute to taste.
- Pour the ginger turmeric golden milk into a mug.
- Enjoy the soothing and flavorful golden milk.

Nutritional Information:

- Calories: 60 kcal
- Sodium: 150 mg
- Potassium: 80 mg

GREEN SMOOTHIE WITH SPINACH, PINEAPPLE, AND COCONUT WATER

Time: 5 minutes

Servings: 1

Ingredients:

- 1 cup fresh spinach leaves
- 1/2 cup frozen pineapple chunks
- 1/2 cup coconut water (low-potassium)
- 1/2 cup water
- Ice cubes (optional)
- Sugar substitute (optional)

Directions:

- In a blender, add the fresh spinach leaves, frozen pineapple chunks, coconut water, and water.

- Blend until smooth and creamy.
- Optionally, add ice cubes for a chilled smoothie.
- If desired, sweeten the smoothie with a sugar substitute.
- Pour the green smoothie into a glass.
- Enjoy the nutritious and refreshing green smoothie.

Nutritional Information:

- Calories: 70 kcal
- Sodium: 55 mg
- Potassium: 420 mg

FRESH LEMONADE (SWEETENED WITH A SUGAR SUBSTITUTE)

Time: 10 minutes

Servings: 2

Ingredients:

- 2 cups water
- Juice of 4 lemons
- Sugar substitute to taste
- Ice cubes (optional)
- Lemon slices for garnish (optional)

Directions:

- In a pitcher, combine water and freshly squeezed lemon juice.
- Add sugar substitute to taste and stir well to dissolve.
- Optionally, add ice cubes to chill the lemonade.
- Pour the fresh lemonade into glasses.
- Garnish with lemon slices, if desired.
- Sip and enjoy the tangy and refreshing fresh lemonade.

Nutritional Information:

- Calories: 10 kcal
- Sodium: 5 mg
- Potassium: 35 mg

28-DAY MEAL PLAN FOR CKD

DAY 1:

Breakfast: Vegetable Egg White Omelet

Lunch: Lentil and Vegetable Curry with Brown Rice

Dinner: Grilled Lemon Herb Chicken with Steamed Broccoli

DAY 2:

Breakfast: Buckwheat Pancakes with Fresh Berries

Lunch: Quinoa Stuffed Bell Peppers with Tomato Sauce

Dinner: Baked Salmon with Dill Sauce and Roasted Asparagus

DAY 3:

Breakfast: Chia Seed Pudding with Almond Milk and Fresh Fruit

Lunch: Grilled Tofu Skewers with Teriyaki Glaze and Grilled Vegetables

Dinner: Turkey Meatballs with Marinara Sauce and Zucchini Noodles

DAY 4:

Breakfast: Greek Yogurt Parfait with Low-Potassium Fruits

Lunch: Shrimp Stir-Fry with Bell Peppers and Snow Peas

Dinner: Vegetable Lasagna with Whole Wheat Noodles and Low-Fat Cheese

DAY 5:

Breakfast: Quinoa Breakfast Bowl with Apples and Cinnamon

Lunch: Lentil and Vegetable Curry with Brown Rice

Dinner: Grilled Pork Tenderloin with Roasted Brussels Sprouts and Sweet Potatoes

DAY 6:

Breakfast: Spinach and Mushroom Frittata

Lunch: Quinoa and Black Bean Salad with Lime Dressing

Dinner: Baked Cod with Lemon and Herbs served with Steamed Spinach

DAY 7:

Breakfast: Oatmeal with Flaxseeds and Sliced Bananas

Lunch: Chicken and Vegetable Stir-Fry with Low-Sodium Soy Sauce

Dinner: Eggplant Parmesan with Whole Grain Spaghetti

WEEK 2:

DAY 8:

Breakfast: Whole Wheat Toast with Avocado and Poached Egg

Lunch: Grilled Tofu Skewers with Teriyaki Glaze and Grilled Vegetables

Dinner: Baked Teriyaki Chicken Thighs with Cauliflower Rice

DAY 9:

Breakfast: Vegetable Egg White Omelet

Lunch: Lentil and Vegetable Curry with Brown Rice

Dinner: Quinoa Stuffed Bell Peppers with Tomato Sauce

DAY 10:

Breakfast: Buckwheat Pancakes with Fresh Berries

Lunch: Shrimp Stir-Fry with Bell Peppers and Snow Peas

Dinner: Grilled Vegetable Skewers with Balsamic Glaze served with Wild Rice

DAY 11:

Breakfast: Chia Seed Pudding with Almond Milk and Fresh Fruit

Lunch: Chicken and Vegetable Stir-Fry with Low-Sodium Soy Sauce

Dinner: Baked Zucchini Boats filled with Ground Turkey and Tomato Sauce

DAY 12:

Breakfast: Greek Yogurt Parfait with Low-Potassium Fruits

Lunch: Quinoa and Black Bean Salad with Lime Dressing

Dinner: Grilled Steak with Portobello Mushrooms and Roasted Green Beans

DAY 13:

Breakfast: Quinoa Breakfast Bowl with Apples and Cinnamon

Lunch: Lentil and Vegetable Curry with Brown Rice

Dinner: Moroccan Chickpea Stew with Couscous

DAY 14:

Breakfast: Spinach and Mushroom Frittata

Lunch: Baked Cod with Lemon and Herbs served with Steamed Spinach

Dinner: Baked Eggplant Rollatini with Ricotta and Marinara Sauce

WEEK 3:

DAY 15:

Breakfast: Oatmeal with Flaxseeds and Sliced Bananas

Lunch: Chicken and Vegetable Stir-Fry with Low-Sodium Soy Sauce

Dinner: Grilled Lemon Herb Chicken with Steamed Broccoli

DAY 16:

Breakfast: Whole Wheat Toast with Avocado and Poached Egg

Lunch: Quinoa and Black Bean Salad with Lime Dressing

Dinner: Vegetable Lasagna with Whole Wheat Noodles and Low-Fat Cheese

DAY 17:

Breakfast: Buckwheat Pancakes with Fresh Berries

Lunch: Grilled Tofu Skewers with Teriyaki Glaze and Grilled Vegetables

Dinner: Baked Salmon with Dill Sauce and Roasted Asparagus

DAY 18:

Breakfast: Chia Seed Pudding with Almond Milk and Fresh Fruit

Lunch: Lentil and Vegetable Curry with Brown Rice

Dinner: Grilled Pork Tenderloin with Roasted Brussels Sprouts and Sweet Potatoes

DAY 19:

Breakfast: Greek Yogurt Parfait with Low-Potassium Fruits

Lunch: Shrimp Stir-Fry with Bell Peppers and Snow Peas

Dinner: Eggplant Parmesan with Whole Grain Spaghetti

DAY 20:

Breakfast: Quinoa Breakfast Bowl with Apples and Cinnamon

Lunch: Quinoa Stuffed Bell Peppers with Tomato Sauce

Dinner: Baked Teriyaki Chicken Thighs with Cauliflower Rice

DAY 21:

Breakfast: Spinach and Mushroom Frittata

Lunch: Grilled Tofu Skewers with Teriyaki Glaze and Grilled Vegetables

Dinner: Lentil and Vegetable Curry with Brown Rice

WEEK 4:

DAY 22:

Breakfast: Oatmeal with Flaxseeds and Sliced Bananas

Lunch: Shrimp Stir-Fry with Bell Peppers and Snow Peas

Dinner: Baked Cod with Lemon and Herbs served with Steamed Spinach

DAY 23:

Breakfast: Whole Wheat Toast with Avocado and Poached Egg

Lunch: Quinoa and Black Bean Salad with Lime Dressing

Dinner: Vegetable Lasagna with Whole Wheat Noodles and Low-Fat Cheese

DAY 24:

Breakfast: Buckwheat Pancakes with Fresh Berries

Lunch: Chicken and Vegetable Stir-Fry with Low-Sodium Soy Sauce

Dinner: Grilled Steak with Portobello Mushrooms and Roasted Green Beans

DAY 25:

Breakfast: Chia Seed Pudding with Almond Milk and Fresh Fruit

Lunch: Lentil and Vegetable Curry with Brown Rice

Dinner: Baked Eggplant Rollatini with Ricotta and Marinara Sauce

DAY 26:

Breakfast: Greek Yogurt Parfait with Low-Potassium Fruits

Lunch: Grilled Tofu Skewers with Teriyaki Glaze and Grilled Vegetables

Dinner: Baked Teriyaki Chicken Thighs with Cauliflower Rice

DAY 27:

Breakfast: Quinoa Breakfast Bowl with Apples and Cinnamon

Lunch: Quinoa Stuffed Bell Peppers with Tomato Sauce

Dinner: Moroccan Chickpea Stew with Couscous

DAY 28:

Breakfast: Spinach and Mushroom Frittata

Lunch: Baked Cod with Lemon and Herbs served with Steamed Spinach

Dinner: Grilled Vegetable Skewers with Balsamic Glaze served with Wild Rice

SNACK OPTIONS:

Cucumber and Tomato Salad with Lemon Dressing

Roasted Beet Chips

Zucchini and Carrot Muffins (low-sodium)

Edamame Hummus with Raw Vegetables

Roasted Chickpeas with Spices

Baked Parmesan Zucchini Rounds

DESSERT OPTIONS:

Quinoa and Black Bean Salad

Fresh Fruit Skewers with Yogurt Dip

Cabbage and Carrot Slaw with Low-Sodium Dressing

Berry and Greek Yogurt Popsicles (low-sugar)

Baked Apple Slices with Cinnamon and Almond Butter

Coconut Milk Rice Pudding with Cardamom

Lemon Poppy Seed Muffins (low-phosphorus)

Mango Sorbet (low-potassium)

Dark Chocolate and Almond Bark (low-sugar)

Greek Yogurt Cheesecake Bites with Fresh Berries

Vanilla Chia Pudding with Sliced Peaches

Cinnamon Baked Pears with Greek Yogurt

Pumpkin Spice Energy Balls (low-phosphorus)

CONCLUSION: LIVING WELL WITH CKD: TIPS FOR LONG-TERM SUCCESS

Living with Chronic Kidney Disease (CKD) can present challenges, but with the right knowledge and lifestyle choices, it is possible to maintain a high quality of life and manage the condition effectively. In this final chapter, we will summarize the key takeaways from this book and provide you with valuable tips for long-term success in managing CKD.

Throughout this book, we have explored the various aspects of CKD, including its causes, symptoms, and complications. We have also discussed the importance of diet, exercise, medication management, and self-care in maintaining kidney health. Armed with this knowledge, let us now focus on practical strategies and tips that will help you lead a fulfilling life while managing CKD.

- Follow a Kidney-Friendly Diet: A healthy diet plays a crucial role in managing CKD. Aim to consume a balanced and kidney-friendly diet that is low in sodium, phosphorus, and potassium. Increase your intake of fresh fruits and vegetables, whole grains, lean proteins, and healthy fats. Limit processed foods, fast foods, and high-sodium condiments. Consult with a registered dietitian who specializes in kidney health to create a personalized meal plan that suits your specific needs.

- Control Blood Pressure and Blood Sugar Levels: High blood pressure and diabetes are common underlying causes of CKD. It is essential to work closely with your healthcare team to monitor and control your blood pressure and blood sugar levels. Take prescribed medications as directed, follow a diabetic diet if necessary, and engage in regular physical activity to manage these conditions effectively.

- Stay Hydrated: Proper hydration is crucial for kidney health. Aim to drink an adequate amount of water throughout the day, unless otherwise advised by your healthcare provider. Keep in mind that excessive fluid intake may be restricted in some cases, depending on your individual needs and the stage of CKD. Consult with your healthcare team for personalized guidance on fluid intake.

- Manage Medications Effectively: It is important to take all prescribed medications as directed by your healthcare provider. Keep a detailed record of your medications, including dosages and schedules. Inform your healthcare team about any over-the-counter medications, herbal supplements, or vitamins you are taking, as they can interact with prescribed medications and impact kidney function.

- Engage in Regular Physical Activity: Regular exercise is beneficial for overall health and can positively impact kidney function. Consult with your healthcare provider before starting any exercise regimen, especially if you have other health conditions. Aim for a combination of aerobic exercises (such as walking, swimming, or cycling) and strength training exercises to maintain muscle mass and cardiovascular health.

- Manage Stress: Chronic stress can have a negative impact on kidney health. Explore stress management techniques such as meditation, deep breathing exercises, yoga, or engaging in hobbies and activities that bring you joy. Seek support from friends, family, or a therapist to help you cope with the emotional challenges that may accompany CKD.

- Monitor and Maintain a Healthy Weight: Obesity and excess weight can put additional strain on the kidneys. Maintaining a healthy weight through a balanced diet and regular physical activity can help reduce the risk of CKD progression. Work with a registered dietitian and a healthcare provider to establish realistic weight loss goals if necessary.

- Regularly Monitor Kidney Function: Regular monitoring of kidney function is crucial in managing CKD. This involves regular blood tests to measure creatinine levels, estimated glomerular filtration rate (eGFR), and urine tests to check for protein leakage. Stay informed about your kidney health status and attend regular appointments with your healthcare provider to discuss test results and any necessary adjustments to your treatment plan.

- Build a Support System: Living with CKD can be emotionally challenging. It is important to build a strong support system of family, friends, and healthcare professionals who understand and can provide the support you need. Consider joining support groups or online communities where you can connect with others who are going through similar experiences.

- Educate Yourself and Advocate for Your Health: Knowledge is power when it comes to managing CKD. Educate yourself about the condition, treatment options, and lifestyle modifications that can improve your kidney health. Stay informed about new research and advancements in CKD management. Be an active participant in your healthcare journey, ask questions, and advocate for your health needs.

In conclusion, managing CKD requires a multifaceted approach that encompasses diet, exercise, medication management, and self-care. By following the tips outlined in this book and working closely with your healthcare team, you can take control of your kidney health and lead a fulfilling life despite the challenges of CKD. Remember, you are not alone in this journey, and with the right knowledge and support, you can live well and thrive with CKD.

Printed in Great Britain
by Amazon

43329749R00089